JEPPESTOWN

Also available from Jeppestown Press

Where the Lion Roars: An 1890 African Colonial Cookery Book

The Bulawayo Cookery Book and Household Guide

The Anglo-African Who's Who 1907

Matabeleland and the Victoria Falls

With Captain Stairs to Katanga

The Ghana Cookery Book

Cooking in West Africa

The Imperial African Cookery Book

Five-O'-Clock Tea

Fifty Breakfasts

The Rhodesia Civil Service List 1902

The Diary of Edwin Clarke: a police officer in Rhodesia, 1906

www.jeppestown.com

The Autobiography of Eugen Mansfeld

A German settler's life in colonial Namibia

Front cover photograph *Namibia*, with thanks to Simon Murgatroyd.
https://www.flickr.com/photos/nomissimon/

Front cover image: plaque showing the German imperial arms; an inscription on the reverse states that it hung in the Post Office at Lüderitzbucht until it was taken as a souvenir by Major F. A. Jones of the First South African Infantry Brigade in October 1915.

Rear cover image: Eugen Mansfeld in his sitting room at Spitzkopje, c1901.

Translation copyright © Jeppestown Press 2017
Published by Jeppestown Press, London. www.jeppestown.com

ISBN 978-0-9570837-5-2 – Hardcover
ISBN 978-0-9570837-4-5 – Paperback

The Autobiography
of Eugen Mansfeld

A German settler's life in colonial Namibia

Translated by Will Sellick

JEPPESTOWN

Contents

Introduction and acknowledgements

In the summer of 1942 Eugen Mansfeld, then aged 71 and living with his daughter-in-law in Cape Town, painstakingly typed out his autobiography; in German, double-spaced on 179 pages of lined paper. He pasted in some family photographs, drew some maps by hand with a fine mapping pen, then bound it all in a hardboard folder and apparently never looked at it again. The original document—a together with Mansfeld's dress sword and war medals, and several folders filled with original documents relating to the Mansfeld family—is in the collection of Dr Nigel McLean of Johannesburg, South Africa.

Mansfeld was a participant in many key events in colonial-era Namibian history. As an early German colonist and employee—later deputy director—of the *Deutsche Kolonial Gesellschaft für Süd West Afrika (DKG)* he was directly involved in the process of appropriation of Namibian land from the people who lived there. He fought against the Herero uprising, issued licences to white diamond prospectors in the early 1900s, and mobilised against British and South African forces as an officer in the *Schutztruppe* Reserve during the First World War.

It is clear from the content and the differing styles within the account that in writing it, Mansfeld drew on other personal, contemporaneous sources: his accounts of the Herero uprising and the First World War are obviously straight transcriptions, more or less, from his original diaries written in the field.

Mansfeld's eventual intention was that his sons should read this book after his death, and a large part of its historical value comes directly from it being a gossipy, informal account by a man writing for his family, not a carefully-considered work for publication or eventual public dissemination. The account makes for a brutal, distressing and uncomfortable read at times (Dr Martha Akawa, a historian at the University of Namibia, describes it as 'stomach-churning', adding that it is 'emotionally draining and plainly upsetting and distressing'.) Constant racism and anti-Semitism; accounts of hanging black combatants during the Herero uprising; a detailed description of how his men set fire to the church and houses of the people of Barmen and the village of Okamita; burning the possessions of a group of Bushmen because Mansfeld believed they had stolen his horses. In one gruesome passage Mansfeld gives a matter-of-fact account of robbing a grave in order to obtain an old man's skull as a souvenir, later boiling the flesh off the skull in the farmhouse kitchen at Spitzkopje and causing Mansfeld's housekeeper to leave in disgust.

First-person accounts of Namibia's complex history are few and far between; this work helps to fill some of the gaps in our understanding of the story of this region of southern Africa. Ultimately the value of Mansfeld's autobiography lies in the new light it enables historians to cast on Namibia's early colonial-era history: in the words of President Hage Geingob, 'gathering and preserving the different eras in history that shaped Namibia into the country it is today'.

My sincere thanks to Christine Leist for her assistance with some particularly idiomatic nineteenth-century German slang phrases; to the Namibian historian Theophelus Gurirab for his assistance in identifying Mansfeld's housekeeper; and to Jan-Bart Gewald for his thoughtful and encouraging suggestions. All translation errors are my own.

Will Sellick
June 2017

Early life

Early life

I have set down the following notes containing an account of my life for my sons, so that after my death they know the story of their father's 'gypsy life'.

I will briefly go over my early youth; it was not all sunny, and my children have had a happier and more loving childhood than I did.

I was born on 1 April 1871 in Tetschen an der Elbe[1] (Bohemia), which was then a proper German provincial town with a population of about 5,000; the second son of Carl Mansfeld, a businessman and Prussian citizen. I lived with my four brothers under the tender care of my parents until my tenth year. Following four years at school in Tetschen, I joined my elder brother Alfred in Dresden both at the *Neustädter Gymnasium* there; and at the austere boarding-house of retired *Grenadier-Feldwebel* Förster, which was run along strictly military lines. After completing a three-year course at the Dresden Higher Business School, on 1 April 1888 I became an apprentice in the office of the Cretuznach & Scheller textile spinning mill, subsequently completing a two-year apprenticeship, and about a year as a clerk. As part of getting to know the technical spinning operation, for a year I was active in the factory from six to nine in the morning, becoming a master spinner, and acquiring engineering knowledge that would prove useful in later years.

On 1 April 1891 I signed up for one year as a volunteer in the *Schützen-Füsilier-Regiment Nr. 108*; I became a *Gefreiter* on 1 October 1891, and was promoted to *Unteroffizier* on 1 January 1892. Shortly after my discharge at the end of March 1892, I got a position at the wool merchants Wilkens & Co. in Antwerp; I used a two-month vacation in 1894 to undertake a one-week military exercise with my regiment, and, promoted to *Vice-Feldwebel*, returned to my firm for another year.

---

[1] Now known as Děčín, in the Czech Republic

These three years in Antwerp counted as the happiest and most carefree of my life. I had a bunch of good friends in Antwerp's German community, and by working hard during my spare time I learned to speak French perfectly; I also spent many happy hours with Walloon and Flemish families. To describe everything would fill a book by itself: looking back, it is probably better if the many stupid pranks we played stay unrecorded.

In March 1895 I returned to Germany to carry out my two eight-weekly Reserve exercises, back with the *Schützen-Füsilier-Regiment*, travelling around in Germany and Austria and participating for a short while in my father's business. But Germany did not attract me: Antwerp was my first taste of a foreign country, and now I felt compelled to travel further afield.

During these military exercises I already carried around references from my boss in Antwerp, Herr Wilkens; and I had applied for positions in Buenos Aires, Montevideo, Sydney and South Africa. I had already had a job offer from Montevideo, which I declined because of the low salary, but I accepted an offer from the firm of Malcomess & Company, in East London in South Africa, as an assistant wool buyer, and I gave notice to Wilkens.

The choice was free passage and a three-year contract; or travel at my own expense, with no contract and one month's mutual notice. "Three years is a long time," I said to myself; "you might prosper, but perhaps you can also find something better while you're in Africa ..." so I declined a contract. My father opposed my travelling to Africa, calling me an 'adventurer', and refused to give or advance me the money for the journey. However, since childhood I had put money in a savings account, which by now also contained my grandfather's inheritance of 300 marks: it went straight towards my travel expenses, and I landed in East London with four pounds in my pocket.

In August 1895 I proceeded to London and introduced myself to the agents of Malcomess & Co.; two days later I was leaving Southampton on board the old Union Castle steamer *Norham Castle*. The journey was uneventful; I never became seasick, and I enjoyed my life and my freedom. I would just like to mention three good pieces of advice that one traveller—an old Scot, with whom I became slightly drunk—offered. He told me that nobody makes a job for you; you must make it for yourself; and to watch out, because in South Africa there are more cheats than honest men.

"One: never talk too much, but listen to what people say; even if they believe you are not listening; and always keep one eye open. Two: you can always make a living using your head, even if somebody else owns your arse. Persevere when you first start out; if you find a good position, stick with it rather than changing jobs when someone offers you a pound more. Three: assume that every man you meet is a swindling bastard until you can convince yourself that he is a genuinely decent chap."

I have always followed this advice, and profited by it; except that years later, in 1922, I did not obey point three—not believing or suspecting that the German homeland could have degenerated so far—and was seriously ripped off.

East London was at that time still a nice little town, the chief harbour for wool exports besides Port Elizabeth. The firm Malcomess & Co. was one of the biggest trading houses, with more than 60 employees in various different departments. There were three men in the Wool Department with plenty to do during the wool season (especially as the senior wool buyer was ill over a long period) as we were buyers for the largest German wool merchants, spinners and laundries, and also for firms in London and Antwerp.

My knowledge of English improved as quickly as possible; I was living with an English family, in which I was the only German out of six other boarders. At precisely the same time, the notorious Jameson Raid took place, leading to the Boer War. Because of the Kaiser's telegram to President Kruger, the mood towards Germany became quite hostile, and I had many a punch thrown at me—but never failed to return the compliment.

The wool season did not give me free weekends; on Monday at noon the European post went from East London, and I wrote weekly wool reports for London, often as long as twenty pages. On Saturdays I sat alone at the office until late on Saturday evening or even Sunday morning, and then on Sunday afternoon brought my report to old Mr Malcomess's[2] house for his signature. Apart from my old friend Jungheinrich, who was manager of the Agricultural Machinery department, I was the only employee to visit the Malcomess home regularly, and I spent many enjoyable Sundays there.

I first learnt to ride in East London. An Afrikaner colleague from work, whose father kept a number of horses, put one always at my disposal. There was one young, fiery beast which went through many a time with me, and repeatedly threw me... I was soon confident in the saddle. My friend and I frequently bought horses, fed them up and groomed them, exercised them, and then sold them for a nice profit, so our financial positions gradually improved. One travelling circus raffled off a horse in a lottery; we bought it the same evening from the winner for two pounds. It was a decrepit old circus-pony, skinny and slouching. We fed it a dose of arsenic, and it soon became beautiful: it fattened up, got a beautiful glossy coat and regained some of its spirit. I used to ride it through the streets in the evening, and it soon aroused the attention of a wealthy Jew, a pig-ignorant wretch who knew nothing of horses, but wanted "ze pretty horsie" for his son Moses. For a long time we pretended to prize the noble animal too much to sell it, and the asking price kept rising until one evening we agreed to sell it. We groomed the old creature so that it gleamed like a mirror; poured a glass of champagne into its nostril to give it bright eyes; shoved two chewed peppercorns into its back passage to keep the long, well-combed tail beautifully high; then I rode it backwards and forwards and put it through its paces.

Our buyer was delighted to carry off the horse, and we shared the proceeds of £27 between us. The noble animal soon became once again a tired, skinny old circus-pony, as its new master naturally did not know our secret methods of feeding and maintaining it.

---

[2] Hermann Malcomess (1848-1921). Malcomess was a German migrant and served as German consul in East London. The engineering firm he founded still exists.

In the middle of 1906 I managed to get a serious attack of typhoid; for four weeks I lay in the hospital, and the doctor gave me up as lost. When I was discharged I weighed only ninety pounds, and was supposed to go home for a change of air and to convalesce; on the suggestion of Herr Malcomess I went to Tilden[3], so that if I wanted to I could assist the branch manager, who was not a wool specialist, with purchasing wool. There we rode out to all the surrounding farms and bought the fleeces—many of which were still on the sheep. For the first eight hours the long ride there and back, at a half-trot, vibrated right into my bones; I had to take off my underwear and riding breeches in the bath, because I had ridden the entire skin of my buttocks raw, and for the following days I had to have my meals standing up, because it was impossible to sit down.

My hospital and medical expenses (which I had to pay for myself as Malcomess & Co did not feel obliged to) ate up my savings again. Malcomess was in Germany and Dirks (his partner at that time) was an unpleasant man, loved and esteemed by none of the company's employees.

I soon saw that life with the wool firms was exactly like being on board a ship: the first buyer is the captain; takes a good salary; buys wool and does nothing more. The second buyer is the first officer; takes a small salary, does the remaining dirty work, and must also often cover the duties of the first buyer. These first buyers are naturally keen to stay in their good positions, and the second buyer can only be promoted if the first buyer should leave or die. Since our first buyer was still a young man like myself, I would not have succeeded to his post until I was a grandfather.

The company turned down an application I put in for a salary increase, and so I said to myself, "Move on, gypsy-boy, and find another trough to feed from". I had already been offered one opportunity: my older brother Alfred had completed his studies and become a doctor of medicine, and was serving as a ship's doctor for one journey on board the steamer *Melita Bohlen*. His destination at that time was Walvis Bay,

---

[3] Near Queenstown in the Eastern Cape

where he was spending three days as the guest of Herr Josef Sichel, of the firm Mertens & Sichel. He had heard from Sichel that the company was looking for an employee in Walvis Bay, and wrote to me: "If East London no longer satisfies you, write immediately to Sichel and tell him when you can start. It's all arranged—let's go to South-West Africa!"

Two years in Walvis Bay

Two years in Walvis Bay

At that time there was no direct steamship route between East London and South-West Africa. I had to travel by railway, to Cape Town via De Aar, where I arrived on 2 January 1897. From here, every month, the small coaster *Leutwein*, 168 tons gross, owned by *Oberleutnant* Troost of Berlin and commanded by Captain Parow, left for Walvis Bay. We departed on the evening of 3 January, with four passengers; travelling with me were George and Ruby Ehlers of the English Guano Company, which had leased Cape Cross[4] from the German Colonial Company.

In their company was a Mr Matthews,[5] who was said to have discovered the guano deposits; he had gone somewhat native, and was a total drunk, but otherwise a good-natured chap. I had the fortune to share one of the two cabins with him: this was no great pleasure in a confined space, as Matthews, to whom the journey was routine, and who did not change his grubby clothes once during the trip, smelled rather strong; and drank two bottles of whisky every night, which he kept hidden in the base of his bunk. After four long days we arrived in Walfisch Bay, and my employment with Mertens & Sichel began immediately.

I was not exactly overwhelmed by the sight of my new home, and it was somewhat different from East London. On a flat plain stood a church and five houses, built from wood and corrugated iron. One of these, the government building, was occupied by Magistrate Cleverly[6] and family, and a white policeman. Then the warehouse and living quarters, with a lean-to, of the company Mertens & Sichel (Sichel[7] and

---

[4] Cape Cross was the site of a stone cross erected by the fifteenth century navigator Diego Câo, and was noted for its huge deposits of guano.

[5] Walter Matthews (d.1899), the itinerant explorer who first discovered and exploited the Cape Cross guano deposits.

[6] John James Cleverly (1856-1906).

[7] Joseph Sichel (1856-1921).

his white manager); in the same building lived an Englishman with his Baster[8] wife. The double-storey house of the harbourmaster, Koch (him, his wife and daughter), and the mission house (Eich and his two daughters). So, generally speaking, following my arrival there were thirteen white adults; while the native population of three hundred Hottentots[9] lived about five kilometres to the east, behind the sand dunes, at the watering-place Sandfontein.

Walvis Bay was the harbour for South-West Africa; almost all goods for the interior had to be landed here, and carried further inland by ox waggon. From the end of 1896 a Wörmann[10] steamship came every two months from Hamburg, with a stop at Swakopmund to unload goods using landing boats.

My home at M&S was a fenced yard of four square metres, made from corrugated iron and crate planks; it contained an iron bedstead, a crate with a wash-basin, and a coat-hook. There were so many draughts coming through the planks and door that my clothing and bed-clothes were usually quite damp from the fog.

Every morning at five o'clock, ox-waggons appeared on the plain behind Walvis Bay. As soon as they became visible from my look-out, I rode out to meet them and buy up their produce—beef oxen, sheep, hides, fleeces and ostrich feathers—before our English competitor in his shed had rubbed the sleep from his eyes and combed the whisky fumes of the previous evening out of his hair. Unloading the waggons and calculating the English customs paperwork and payments for the freight drivers, whose transport costs came out of the sale proceeds, took until late in the evening. Only then could I carry out the remaining work—correspondence and book-keeping.

In March 1897 a sailing ship from Argentina brought Herr Otto Bohnstedt and his wife, with 120 horses for their farm. There was still no jetty, and the horses had to be landed on rafts. Bohnstedt

---

[8] A Namibian ethnic group of mixed African and European heritage.

[9] A derogatory name for the Khoekhoe people of southern Africa.

[10] Wörmann was a major German shipping line operating between Hamburg and German colonies in Africa.

thought he was being clever by buying a number of pregnant mares, hoping that they would foal soon after arriving at the farm. During the course of the two-month voyage the animals had suffered terribly from sea-sickness, had been thrown back and forth and maltreated, and most had miscarried as a consequence. While I was down on the raft beside the sailors, standing by a number of horses waiting to disembark, it was terrible to see one mare giving birth while left hanging in a sling. The whole undertaking was an utter fiasco; these mares were naturally useless for further breeding purposes; still more animals died on the long overland trek to the farm; and Bohnstedt's horse breeding ended with this expensive experiment.

Shortly afterwards, a steamship arrived with three hundred geldings from Argentina for the German troops in South West, which we had to land in the same way. For the most part these were beautiful animals; but also unbroken, perfectly wild, malicious devils. However, by dint of hard work and much struggling—and a few blows—we brought them all ashore safely.

Sichel was known across the region for his hospitable, open house, and as a result we enjoyed many visits from officers of the garrison and other company owners from Swakopmund, going on late into the night. In the evenings I was often in the family home of the magistrate, Cleverly, who was always happy to find someone to join him in a whisky and soda; I sometimes used to ride on Sundays with his three eldest daughters, young women of thirteen to fifteen years but, unsurprisingly, life in Walvis Bay was, generally speaking, tedious and dull.

The missionary, Eich, a former shoemaker, was extremely pious, and regarded each native as a 'brother', living with us in perfect harmony. His two daughters were prim spinsters, and it was impossible to have a convivial conversation with them.

Ludwig Koch, the tubby little harbourmaster, was a reliable and very sociable man, who had a strong interest in native folklore, and was even to be found every Sunday in church for the native service. A young English official, who was stationed in Walvis Bay for a short time, joined me in playing a practical joke on Koch. On the evening of

Christmas Day 1897, when Koch was in church, we brought one of the little cart-donkeys into his house; up the steep stairs to the first floor and into his bedroom, and quickly tied it to the door-handle (the door opened outwards). Now, after midnight, Koch, with the sinister preaching of the missionary about the devil's evil works preying on his mind, came back to his house half-asleep and tried to open his bedroom door. The donkey began to bray loudly and Koch nearly died from fright. Believing that Satan had arrived to claim his soul, he flew down the stairs in search of the help and protection of the missionary.

Carrying lanterns, and armed with sticks, Koch, the missionary and his daughters crept into the open house and discovered the joke that had been played on him. It never came out who had done it, as the Englishman and I swore that we had been tucked up in our beds since ten o'clock that evening; therefore the devil was assumed to have had some part in the prank. Already it had not been easy to push the donkey up the stairs; it was equally hard to persuade him back down, and this took up several hours of Boxing Day morning.

In July 1897 I cut my right hand on the lining while unpacking a tin-lined crate, and developed such serious blood-poisoning that I had to visit the doctor in Swakopmund, because there was none in Walvis Bay. There was no railway; the steamer service was two months away; the only way to travel the forty kilometres to Swakopmund was on foot or horseback. Sichel had at his place an old mare called Liese to fetch the fresh water from Sandfontein every day in a water-cart. I knew that good old Liese was not exactly a racehorse, but needs must in an emergency! I therefore rode her gently, and even though I was not able to persuade her to great speed, she brought me to Swakopmund by evening, nevertheless.

I immediately went off to be patched up, and stayed there overnight; and the following day the gentle little medical officer again thoroughly cleaned up the hand, dressed it and put it in a sling which I tied again myself on the journey back. Though it was a long time ago, I have never forgotten this journey. Liese was all but finished, and could barely walk, stumbling continuously. When we were about ten kilometres from Swakopmund she simply lay down. I took off her saddle, slung it on my back, laid her bridle over my arm and trudged through the heavy sand, pulling Liese behind me, for the thirty kilometres to Walvis Bay. It took eight hours.

At the beginning of 1898 Sichel returned to Germany. I managed the entire business on my own for eight months. When Sichel returned, Georg Schluckwerder came with him as partner; Schluckwerder wanted the company run his way, and I noticed that I was being pushed aside, as he was keen to bring his brother into the business. I left the firm on 20 December 1898 and took the steamer *Leutwein* to Cape Town in order to acquire with my savings a net-curtain business which I had seen offered there. The journey began to get lively right after our departure from Walvis Bay, in a strong south-westerly storm and heavy seas which left the small steamer (which was without cargo) rolling, bouncing and dancing, so that the lower deck was constantly underwater.

I was the only passenger, and the only place on deck where I could stay was on the bridge, next to the captain's cabin. The ship had a steering wheel on the bridge, and at eleven o'clock at night the pitching and rolling of the sea caused four teeth to snap off the steering mechanism. As a consequence, the only possible emergency remedy was to control the chain which attached the steering wheel to the rudder, pulled by hand by sailors on each side.

Naturally, the ship rolled in every direction, but without letting the seas crash against the length of the vessel, which would have simply capsized the ship. As sleep was obviously impossible, Captain Parow and I spent the night on the bridge, and kept ourselves awake by drinking one hot toddy after another. Better to go under drunk than sober—for none of us believed that we would see land again—until at four o'clock the next morning we reached the uninhabited Hottentot Bay, as though delivered to a place of refuge. There emergency repairs were carried out to the steering rudder and, after the weather had settled down, we set out on our journey twenty-four hours later, and reached Cape Town on 24 December at eight o'clock at night.

We could not dock: the Anglo-Boer War had broken out, and all the wharves were piled high with all sorts of supplies for the troops, and guards stood everywhere. It was Christmas Eve and I wanted to land. However, Parow of course refused permission. After he had gone to bed, I bribed a sailor with £1 to carry me in a small boat to the quay wall. Carefully, avoiding all the alert guards, I climbed over the various iron railings, and was in the city by ten o'clock. When the *Leutwein* tied up right next to the quay, I managed to smuggle myself back on board with the Customs and immigration inspectors and return to the vessel unobserved, so that my informal landing was unnoticed.

If I had been superstitious, I would have had to regard this arduous journey as a bad omen for my new plans, and would have had second thoughts.

It was a short but painful fiasco. I fell into the hands of two sophisticated con-artists. A credit account which I needed for the business was opened to me by a wholesale supplier, but then closed under the pettiest possible circumstances. While investigating the obligations of the business, which I was to inherit, I uncovered further liabilities of the previous owner which would quickly have bankrupted me. I therefore withdrew myself from the whole mess in the quickest possible time. However, I had incurred brokers' and transfer fees, and was bled for a share of the agreed goodwill payment, which used up the savings from Walvis Bay which I had painfully acquired.

I applied for various jobs in Johannesburg, Rhodesia and Bechuanaland, but one effect of the Anglo-Boer War was to block chances for my employment at English companies. I sent a letter to the General Representative of the *Deutsche Kolonial Gesellschaft für Süd West Afrika*,[11] Dr Rhode,[12] who knew me from Walvis Bay, and received a reply at the beginning of April 1899: "You are engaged, come by next available steamer, fare paid."

And so I was once again saved from poverty; at the time I never suspected that I would remain in the service of the company for 22½ years.

---

[11] *DKG*, the German Colonial Society for Southwest Africa—this colonial exploration company held a monopoly on most mineral rights in the region.
[12] Dr Max Rhode.

Working for the *DKG*

Working for the *DKG*

The *Deutsche Kolonial Gesellschaft für Süd West Afrika* (*DKG*) had succeeded to the rights of F.A.E. Lüderitz of Bremen, owners of the whole area from the Orange River up to Kunene, twenty German miles inland, and holder of the mineral rights in these regions and in Hereroland, which made it the largest German colonial company. The rights were established in contracts that the Lüderitz company had signed with different native chiefs, and had been challenged several times and confirmed by the German government. Land and farms had to be acquired through the Company agent in Swakopmund, and prospecting licences for all sorts of minerals and ores, as well as the exploitation rights, had to be obtained and delivered in Swakopmund.

On my arrival in Swakopmund Dr Rhode told me that he did not have a suitable position for me at that time, but had been keen to secure my services. I spent three weeks in Swakopmund employed in learning stocktaking, and was then placed at the farm Spitzkopje, 135 kilometres north-east of Swakopmund. The manager there, Schlettwein,[13] had to travel as a representative to an agricultural show in Windhoek, and I remained behind so that Frau Schlettwein and their two children were not left alone at the farm.

Spitzkopje was a company farm of 120,000 hectares on the edge of the Namib desert. It had good rainfall, fine pasture and sufficient water for at least two years. Spitzkopje was a horse stud, with about 120 mares and good, imported stallions; it was stocked with about 1,500 cattle, dairy cows and oxen, about 4,000 sheep and goats, and additional pigs and fowl. On the farm there was a five-room farmhouse built of stone, with a kitchen, dairy and farm store. About thirty metres away were outbuildings including a stable, storeroom, harness-room and smithy. The farmworkers and cattlemen were natives, Hereros, Bergdamaras and Hottentots, who lived with their extended families about 150 metres beyond the outbuildings. The operations of the farm

---

[13] Carl Schlettwein (1866-1940), a leading representative of the settler community.

were naturally something new for me, but I enjoyed it and quickly mastered all my duties.

Schlettwein had one white worker on the farm, a Pole; a hulking, ignorant brute who did not understand how to deal with the native workers, and whom they hated. One day in the smithy he beat one kaffir and gave him a bloody head wound, at which all the natives present stopped their work and explained to me that they did not want to continue working under the man. I managed to calm the people down by assuring them that they would subsequently receive instructions only from me. I sent the Pole back to Schlettwein, for assignment to different work in which he would come into contact with no natives.

The latter was unnecessary. Just three days later he became seriously ill, with symptoms of intoxication; he died after a further three days—poisoned, without a doubt. The natives use deadly plants, which are undetectable in the corpse of a dead man; although I had my suspicions of the killer's identity, the culprit was never discovered. It was the first time that I had played gravedigger, and I even made a coffin out of old packing-case planks, something the natives were conspicuously unwilling to give me any assistance with.

When Schlettwein returned from Windhoek after about five weeks, he commissioned me to take a cart with twelve oxen and three natives to Franzfontein, about 220 kilometres north of Spitzkopje. An Afrikaner there had failed to pay off his massive credit balance at the farm store, and I was to collect cash or bring back cattle in payment. Schlettwein did not know the distance to Franzfontein, and believed that I would get there in three days. He measured out the provisions which he gave us accordingly, and if I had not shot buck on the way we would have gone hungry on our journey, because it took twelve days over appalling roads, in deep sand through dry river beds, uphill and downhill over mountains.

One night we outspanned near a waterhole in a ravine in the Khorikas mountains because we had lost the precise course of the road in the darkness; we were awakened by the dreadful roar of lions, which we discovered the next morning were nearby at the waterhole. Our draught oxen panicked, and we had a tough job calming them down again.

In Franzfontein I stayed for three days meeting with Sabatta,[14] and gradually persuaded him to pay 30 beautiful fat oxen as instalments to clear his debt so that I could go back to Spitzkopje.

Soon after my return I was called back to Swakopmund to take over harbour management there for the Company. A harbour jetty or mole did not yet exist in Swakopmund at that time; the normal heavy surf usually caused the steamships to anchor two to three nautical miles from the beach, and all goods had to be brought ashore in open surf-boats, if the swell was not too heavy. The harbour management was shared between the *DKG*, the Damara and Namaqua Commercial Company, and the Walvis Bay harbour agent Koch, all under a white manager who was called the Beach-Pirate-General. The DKG had for its trade seven large surf-boats, staffed by sixty Kru men from West Africa, under their headman Meyer, and in addition employed about 120 Hereros, Ovambos and Kaffirs at the port.

Often boats capsized in the waves, and then it meant me, and three or four natives roped behind me, plunging into the water in order to save the boat crew. Many brave Kru men were drowned in this way, and I was also once nearly drowned myself. A steamer had finished loading, and the sea had become very rough. Further communication with the ship hardly seemed possible but, since the ship wanted to leave, the ship's papers still had to be taken on board. Following consultation with the Kru headman, I dared try it in the late afternoon with a boat directed by him through the increasingly tumultuous waves. Luckily we reached the steamer, but on the return journey with six men rowing and me steering, the boat stood on its head just three waves from shore. The six men flew away forward over the waves. However, I, sitting right at the very rear of the boat, was thrown behind the waves. Despite swimming with all my strength, I could not swim beyond the crest of the wave, and was thrown back again and again. It was futile to seek help from land, and after about fifteen minutes I dived between two

---

[14] Probably Edward Sabatta (1854-1917), who is buried at Karibib Cemetery.

waves and, even as I thought I would drown, with a fresh effort came to the crest of the wave, throwing me into the shallows, from where four hands caught and pulled me ashore.

There was a drive to build the first railway in Southwest in these years; a narrow-gauge railway of sixty centimetres from Swakopmund to Windhoek via Karibib. In addition, all the railway materials had to be landed in this fashion: each surf-boat was loaded with thirty to fifty rails or sixty to one hundred sleepers; the boats approached through the waves and presented themselves lengthways to the beach, then often tilted, and the rails were lost in the sea water and swirling sand. For us that was a quick and effortless unloading of the boat: hundreds of rails were lost in this way. Six locomotives also had to be landed. One of the biggest steam boilers ever was shipped on a surf-boat, and brought with the high tide so far up the beach that it sat on dry land once the tide ebbed away; and then I proceeded to land all the locomotives safely by means of an apparatus of tripods and pulleys and railway track, planned in the course of one sleepless night. This brought me a special commendation from the railway commander and a beautiful cash bonus from the Company.

The Hereros and Ovambos contracted pneumonia from the cold and foggy air, and there were many injuries from unloading the boats, so we set up our own hospital. As I was of course responsible for the health and welfare of the natives employed in landing operations, I always accompanied the Company doctor on his daily rounds to learn as much as I could about sickness, diagnosis and medical operations, and often used the information later.

At the beginning of February 1900 I was replaced at my landing post and sent to the Salem Company horticulture station in Swakopmund to make a full audit of the books, since the manager there was suspected of embezzlement. I was there for fourteen really unpleasant days. The manager, who had previously been for a long time in Argentina, was a drunken bully who, when he noticed that I had uncovered his theft, became even drunker and threatened to shoot me. The two of us were alone on the Salem station, but about three kilometres away was a police station occupied by a police noncommissioned officer who came one evening by chance—and luck—to the farmhouse and straightened out the situation directly.

The manager was drunk again, and standing with a loaded rifle in front of the open window of the room in which I worked, making loud remarks about bringing eternal rest to people who looked too closely into his books. I went toward him and ordered him to put the rifle away immediately. He just grinned at me scornfully, I pulled a loaded revolver from my pocket and, before he could make a move with the rifle, pointed it at his chest and cried "Hands up!"

At the same moment the police officer, whose presence I had been unaware of, but who had witnessed the manager's threats, sprang forward out of the darkness, grabbed the manager from behind and put handcuffs on him. At my request he took the manager to the police station and locked him up overnight. When I came to the station the next morning, my colleague had sobered up, and was weeping and whimpering for mercy. With the agreement of the police officer, I told him that I would not lay charges against him if he immediately packed his things and cleared out of Swakopmund. He did; I do not know where he went, but I have never seen him again.

On my return to Swakopmund I heard that the Company was planning an expedition to discover guano deposits along the coast up to the Orange River. The search was to be made by camel and mule, and would include the purchase of a yacht that would precede the expedition, depositing provisions, fodder and water at different places on the coast. I wanted to lead the land expedition. Dr Rhode asked me the following day whether I thought I was capable of it, and I simply replied, "Yes". He ordered me to take the steamship *Leutwein*, leaving Swakopmund the next day for Cape Town, and entrusted me to look out there for a good, suitable yacht, and to purchase it. I was to return on the steamer *Gertrud Wörmann* eight days later, and to bring along three hundred Angora goats for Spitzkopje farm.

I had naturally enough no idea what sort of yacht to look for, only that I had a budget of 10,000 marks, but I thought "Don't be afraid", and with the help and expert advice of my old friend Captain Parow and the captains of two large sailing boats at anchor in Cape

Town, I bought a yacht and ordered its captain and crew to head for Swakopmund. The three hundred Angora goats were of course transported from the interior by train, and once these were loaded on board the *Gertrud Wörmann*, I went back to Swakopmund.

The yacht arrived in Swakopmund as planned, was fitted out and one afternoon set out to begin its coastal trip. The captain, a little Irishman, was not a drunkard; but he was a religious maniac, and prayed constantly. I am a long way from asserting that he was to blame for the accident, but after four days the message reached us that he had anchored the ship overnight near Sandwich Harbour so close to the coast that it had been wrecked on the cliffs, with the loss of all hands. As a result, Berlin's enthusiasm for the guano expedition diminished, and it was abandoned.

Dr Rhode, who I noted was charitable, already had other posts for me. I heard from a third party that he had said: "I want to keep testing Mansfeld until the day he says 'No, I can't do that; I don't dare do that'". However, he never heard me say that. Berlin had reserved a sum of money for the acquisition of young cows and heifers for the farm Heusis in the Khomas highlands; so that became my new responsibility, and of course I said yes to it.

"How many cows, where and how you acquire them and what price you pay for them is down to you," is all Dr Rhode said to me, "and after that… away you go!" For myself I ordered from Spitzkopje a cart with twelve oxen, five natives and a horse to Rössing Station; and over the course of three months collected altogether approximately six hundred cows and heifers from various different farms around the district, in each case having them delivered by the seller to Heusis in herds of fifty to one hundred head of cattle. Our farm manager at Heusis was a first-class connoisseur of cattle, formerly from Argentina, and it was a source of the greatest satisfaction to me that he reported to Swakopmund that I had bought only top-quality animals, and cheaply; something of which—as a businessman rather than a farmer—he had not thought me capable.

On my return to Swakopmund there was already another call for assistance from Spitzkopje; Sabatta had not paid, and I was to go to see him once again. A mule-cart got me to Spitzkopje, and because I had now travelled quite enough by ox-cart, this time I decided that I would travel only on horseback. I rode quickly, with three good horses, one packhorse and a native, and was in Franzfontein in three-and-a-half days. Only the most necessary stores were packed, of course: a few rusks, a little tea and sugar; a field canteen or small tea-kettle; a little rough tobacco for use as gifts or barter for natives; and a blanket. My rifle and canteen filled with water were always on my own horse. At night I slept in the bush beside the horses, and afterwards left them to graze while I watched; because of the danger of lions in this region horses were kept tethered to a tree at night.

I dealt forcefully with Sabatta. This time I did not stay with him, but on the military station with *Oberleutnant* von François,[15] and after I had, within three days, forced Sabatta to give up the balance of the debt he owed, I rode back to Spitzkopje. When I arrived, Schlettwein was in Swakopmund, where he had a blazing row with Dr Rhode, leading to the termination of his contract. At the same time I received an order for my return to Swakopmund to await further news. Schlettwein returned furious, and rode back over to Swakopmund two days later. It was said that he had challenged Dr Rhode to sack him there and then in the hope of embarrassing Rhode, who had no suitable successor in place. Schlettwein had admittedly not been serious, but Dr Rhode immediately accepted his resignation and sent me a special message: "Schlettwein is going. Remain at Spitzkopje until further notice and take over management of the farm."

Although I was no farmer by vocation, nevertheless I had observed on other farms what I had missed at Spitzkopje. Schlettwein had himself in the last year been over-occupied in writing a book on farm management, how it is and how it should be, and had consequently himself missed out some of the 'how it should be'.

The inadequate old thorn-bush cattle kraal at the farm was falling to pieces, and I therefore built a large new kraal from earthen

---

[15] This is most likely Hugo von François, who was a junior officer in German South-West Africa.

bricks which we fired ourselves. I sorted the stock into large and small animal herds, and in order to relieve pressure on the pastures near the stockyards, allocated herds to outlying watering places, always under the supervision of a reliable native. Only the milk-cows with calves, the imported Friesian cattle, the Angora goats and a selected herd of young female sheep and goats which had not yet been mated, were pastured in the vicinity of the stockyards and brought at night into the cattle kraal at the farm. The mares were kept separately from the stallions and there one year we suffered large losses of foals taken by leopards overnight, so herded the foals at night (sometimes up to sixty of them) with their mothers into special enclosures under guard.

In the evening every herd was counted, so the phrase 'lost in the bush' soon became redundant. Of course, the shepherds often brought in at night a dead sheep that had died of snakebite, or some other illness, but only after the cause of death was identified did they get it for their cooking pot. One shepherd, frustrated that no snake had bitten his charges and no animal dropped dead in the field to satisfy his appetite for fresh meat, helped nature along. He shoved a pointed stick into the sheep's back passage, ripping the intestines so that the poor animal died a miserable death. I discovered this while examining the dead beast; an elderly Baster, who happed to be at the farm, watched and confirmed my diagnosis as an old trick of the natives. Rather than mutton that evening, that shepherd got a proper beating from the biggest cowherd. The other natives shook their heads and said, "The old jackal (as they called me) notices everything."

When all the cattle had been safely returned to the kraal, and all the cows milked, and the natives received their rations from the store, then my day's work was finally over. But often I was woken during the night by a rider from a remote cattle station, with a message that this or that had happened, and then I had to ride there at once.

We lost foals to leopards, sheep to leopards and hyenas, and newborn lambs to the jackals. I shot a lot of these predators, or trapped or poisoned them, and when we knew that a leopard had been prowling round the cattle kraal I would stand guard at night for some hours on watch. Spitzkopje was blessed with all sorts of snakes, especially the black mambas; I killed these creatures on the stoep and even inside the house, while in the rocks behind the house you had to watch out at every step. There was wonderful hunting for buck: kudu, gemsbok (oryx), springbok, steenbok, etc. I rarely even had to slaughter a sheep, but lived mostly on venison.

To look after the farmhouse I had brought in a young Bergdamara woman, a niece of Chief Cornelius,[16] as cook and housekeeper ("not just a kaffir", as Cornelius said), and was looked after accordingly. She was educated at the mission, could read and write, spoke pretty good German, and did an excellent job of looking after the kitchen and the entire household[17]—so that as host, I maintained the reputation of the Company whether looking after guests, farmers, army officers or government officials.

I had a good friendship with Chief Cornelius, which benefited me greatly, for his people had a fearful respect for him. If I was looking for good farm-workers or shepherds, he would bring them to me himself—and woe to those who let him down. Cornelius often used to ride over to me, accompanied by his adjutants; stay two or three days and eat and drink to his heart's content.

At home I had two dogs; a tame sheep, a tame steenbok and a little baboon, so there was always some company. I had also raised two leopards from cubs to maturity, and kept them in a large barred enclosure which I used to go into every day to feed them until one day one of them (the female, of course) took a dislike to my visits and attacked me, and I no longer dared to enter. I sent them to the Zoological Garden in Berlin.

By 1899 I had already contracted malaria, then in the following years had serious attacks, spending a whole week with severe seizures. I often suffered terribly, on my own, with no other white people in the district. In 1903 I left to go to Germany until I had got rid of the illness.

---

[16] King Cornelius Goreseb (1844-1910) of Okombahe, who was installed as a Damara chief by the German administration in 1894.

The nearest doctor was in Swakopmund, 135 kilometres away, so I had to play both doctor and veterinarian. I had to provide maternity care not only to horses and cows but also to one native woman; treated all fever and other illnesses; doctored all the sick and injured myself and once even amputated the finger of a young Herero girl with blood poisoning, without any pain at all. Well, not for me, anyway.

By the end of 1900 Rinderpest had broken out again in the region. They sent me a corporal of the *Schutztruppe* who had been trained in vaccination. Between us we vaccinated six hundred head of stock, and were delighted that we lost only three animals. Every month I was riding out to our largest cattle posts on the edge of the Omaruru River, about sixty kilometres from Spitzkopje, a journey which always took two days and a night.

In Spitzkopje there are very few sources of water; you need to know their exact location. Anyone lost in this country will die of thirst, and before my time several white men died here in this way. One day I met a white man who had come from Swakopmund in an ox-waggon, going to Omaruru. He was half-dead from thirst, and told me that he and his companion had left the waggon and had run on ahead, becoming lost and spending the night alone in the bush. He had already wandered for two days looking for water, and his friend, who had not reappeared, was still lost. I immediately saddled a horse, took water, a small flask of cognac and some food, and rode in the direction of the area where the two men had become separated. After hours of riding backwards and forwards I saw in the dense bush on the back of the Spitzkopje, only about an hour away from the farmhouse, a half-naked figure crawling round. He was immediately hostile in response to my calls, and tried to throw stones at me, but was so weak that he could barely lift them.

I dismounted and went to the man, held him down on the ground and poured water into him sip by sip until he had drunk enough for his head to begin to clear again. After a long while feeding him water, cognac and food I brought the poor fellow back to such a point of normality that he had stopped viewing me as an enemy but as a rescuer. He had spent two days and nights walking round in wide circles. He had gradually become half-mad with thirst, and gradually discarded all his clothes until he had only trousers and a shirt ripped to shreds by thorns and eventually was no longer able to limp on any further. I put him on my horse and, leading it on foot, brought him back to the farm. After three days' rest and care I sent them on their way with an ox-waggon which had by good fortune come to Spitzkopje on its way to Omaruru.

From time to time I had to go in person to Swakopmund, either riding on horseback or by means of a small wheeled cart, drawn by six strong mules, which then rumbled away like a thunderstorm. As there was no water or pasture to be had en route, the journey had to be made in a single trip of 135 kilometres, with regular ten minute breaks, making a rather arduous journey for both man and animals. During this time the farm was left under the supervision of a Baster foreman, and the respect of the natives for their chief's niece guaranteed that the house was not disturbed.

During my stay on Spitzkopje I collected many curios: horns of the various antelope species, mostly shot by myself; Herero, native and Bushman weapons and everyday objects; snake skins and snake skulls prepared with fangs; and skulls of all kinds of animals and the natives of various races. I collected Herero, Bergdamara, Baster, Hottentot and even a Bushman skull. Obtaining a Bushman skull is difficult and dangerous, because if Bushmen were told that one of their dead had been dug up, they would take the strongest possible revenge. Despite that, my desire to get such a skull was stronger than the risk of retribution. One day I heard from the native women that they had seen a grave in the high rocks behind the farmhouse. It was immediately obvious to me that this could only be that of a Bushman, who buried their dead under stones, and who used in earlier times to live on Spitzkopje.

My offers of rewards for getting the skull were rejected in horror by the farm workers, and I was warned that the Bushmen would surely kill me. I wanted to have the skull, so I had to get it myself, in secret, and the same night—for I had to consider betrayal by my own natives, even if they were generally trustworthy.

When the native compound became silent in the late evening, I armed myself with a stick and, taking a lantern, went out and climbed some two hundred metres up the rocks and over huge stone boulders, often on my hands and knees, cautious of snakes in the dark. Eventually I came to the location the women had described, and I found the grave in a cleft in the rocks. First I had to remove the large rocks that covered the grave; that took about an hour's hard work until the skeleton was uncovered and I could remove the skull I coveted.

I wrapped up my prize in a large handkerchief and tied it round my neck, and climbed down carefully. I was bruised and somewhat exhausted, as this grave-robbing expedition had taken some five hours. No natives had seen me; my only witness was the moon, who thankfully did not tell the Bushmen.

However, I could not conceal the boiling of the head night and day on the cooking-stove from my good Hottentot cook. She told me that she would have nothing to do with this escapade, and refused to stay in the house any longer.[18]

When I left Germany in 1928 I lent my entire collection, which later included magnificent specimens of ores and minerals, to the Anthropological School at Wandsbek near Hamburg for their South-West Africa museum. I have retained ownership, however, so I can always get it back. I will probably never use it again, but I wanted my sons to be able to have the collection if any of them express an interest in it.

Apparently Dr Rhode was back with other plans for me, because I received a message from Swakopmund that a trained farm manager had been recruited from Germany and was coming up to Spitzkopje with the waggons that I had just sent down to get provisions, and that I was to hand the entire operation of Spitzkopje over to him. As neither of the waggons was back on the day that I expected them to return, I

---

[18] The oral history of the Gorasen royal house identifies Mansfeld's housekeeper as Christina |Gamiros Goreses, sister of Cornelius Goreseb. She is said to have walked 80km from Spitzkopje to Okombahe when she realised that the mad German at Spitzkopje killed black people and cooked their heads.

took a ride out into the bush, and met one of the natives from the waggons. He reported that both waggons had been outspanned overnight by a river about fifteen kilometres away when the white man they had brought from Swakopmund had disappeared into the darkness; they had heard a shot, and were looking for him.

"What a beautiful mess", I said to myself. It had been made abundantly clear to the passenger that he was not allowed to leave the waggon because he would otherwise become lost and perish in the veld. I rode out immediately. When I reached the outspanned waggons the foreman, a Baster, told me that they had just found the man, dead. They were afraid to go to him, and had waited until I arrived. This was very sensible, because it would otherwise have spoiled the footprints, which I needed to use to establish what had happened. When I questioned the natives they told me that during the whole trip the man was very nervous and withdrawn; that he had not put his gun down for an instant, and had constantly warned them that if they tried anything he would shoot them all. He said that he regretted coming to this dangerous country and wanted to return to Germany immediately.

I slowly followed the man's tracks; they were clear, and led to a small hill covered in bushes. He was lying on his face, gun still in his hand, its muzzle at his right temple; he was dead and already stiff. It was clearly suicide: his words and phrases appeared close to paranoia, and I felt reassured that no hint of suspicion of murder could attach to the workers (all of whom were trusted employees of long standing). The stranger was a man of about thirty-five, a large, powerfully-built figure, and it was not easy to fetch the heavy body from the hill and load it onto the waggon.

I rode back in the evening and met the waggon carrying the body. The next morning we had to hurry to Spitzkopje to bury him immediately, since the corpse was already distended and blown up by the great heat. I then had a lot of work making reports about the events to the Company and the colonial authorities in Swakopmund, as well as writing to his relatives in Germany.

The year 1900 had brought little rain, and as the rainy season from February to April 1901 passed by Spitzkopje without the anticipated downpours, there was not enough grazing there for the cattle, so it was decided to bring most of the animals to Heusis. This wonderful job fell to me again; it was a genuinely enjoyable task but tough, with risks because the pasture and water conditions were very poor and we had just fourteen days to bring the cows, oxen, bullocks and calves to their destination.

I set off with seven mounted cattle-drivers and a bullock cart for food and so on. For days the smallest, weakest calves had to be carried in the waggon. In those days the steep, mountainous track between Otjimbingwe and Heusis was so bad that the waggon overturned twice—but only after we, anticipating the danger-spots, had unloaded the calves and provisions beforehand.

I usually rode ahead to look for watering holes and find places to rest. At one point in the mountains I found excellent pasture, but the local water-hole was dry. The location was framed by steep cliffs about sixty metres high, and on the top I found a pool in the rocks containing plenty of water. To bring the stock up to drink from it was impossible, of course, but they had to drink, and there was nothing for it but to create a sort of waterfall, so to speak, using a bucket and feed bags to pour the water and send it running down the rock walls. It took hours before we had shifted enough water for all the animals.

Every evening when we made camp we had to cut thorn branches to build into a kraal for the animals. Because they were never properly fed and watered, they never stayed quiet, and began to wander, often breaking out of the kraal, so we got very little sleep. You can imagine how happy I was when I was able to deliver my four-legged problem children to Heusis after a fourteen-day march, having lost only three animals on the way.

After two days' rest at Heusis I sent the cart with the natives straight back to Spitzkopje. I rode the following day from Heusis to Windhoek, where I had a number of tasks to carry out for various businesses in Swakopmund. I was invited to the officers' mess several times, which left me very contented. Then the three-day ride back to Spitzkopje.

In Spitzkopje there was only a small number of animals, together with an ox-team and some cows, and a young man was sent from Swakopmund to look after them. I soon received an order to pack my belongings and quickly come to Swakopmund, where I expected to get another posting. And that was the end of my free life as a farmer, to which I have often looked back with nostalgia. I have often wondered how I endured one-and-a-half years alone as the only white man (my nearest white neighbour was about sixty kilometres away at Okombahe) surrounded by natives at Spitzkopje, and if it was not boring, lonely and dangerous. I can only conclude that I never felt bored or scared because the activity on a farm is so varied—from early morning to late evening, offering so many opportunities to create and try out new ideas, plans and improvements. I have realised that anybody who loves and desires this sort of challenge, who enjoys nature and the natural world and can do without the pleasures and comfort of big cities, will probably be happy on a farm.

With natives I have never experienced difficulties or felt anxiety when dealing with them. I have always treated them in a firm but fair way; rewarding and recognising good service and punishing bad. I never participate in pointless violence or name-calling. As obtuse, obstinate and sneaky as the native may often be, he has a fine sense of feeling and understanding so long as one does not simply treat him as a beast of burden and his master understands his worries about his welfare; as well as having sympathy for his customs and traditions and his legitimate aspirations. Treated well, the native is willing to work hard, and to always recognise the white man as his master.

I could not imagine what remote post I would be sent to next. On my arrival in Swakopmund, Dr Rhode informed me that the representative of the Company in Lüderitzbucht[19] had been sent back to Germany with a nervous breakdown; and I had been appointed as Company representative and head of the branch in Lüderitzbucht. So,

---

[19] Mansfeld used the name Lüderitzbucht, which strictly speaking refers only to *Angra Pequena* bay, to refer to the town known as Lüderitz.

something new and entirely different, and I said to myself, "Yes, I'll do it," sailing out on a Wörmann steamship just two days later.

The settlement of Lüderitzbucht consisted of a large warehouse and store, independent of Swakopmund; a coaling station for the Imperial Navy; the only port landing operation for all incoming sea cargo; and water supply by means of a steam condenser, for there was no fresh water in Lüderitzbucht and the surrounding areas. There was no railway, and no telegraphic connection to Swakopmund, Cape Town or the interior. Once a month the steamer *Leutwein* came from Cape Town, and the monthly Wörmann steamer from Hamburg brought mail, but postal communication with outlying districts was only possibly by ox-cart or sending a messenger.

There was a government building, with a station chief and two officers as police officers and customs officials; a Company warehouse and storage sheds with rooms for the employees, and his own house for the Company representative. There was also a warehouse with living accommodation for the companies Seidel & Mühle and Georg Hesselman. The Company had three store and office workers, a machinist for the condensing operation and a Norwegian boatswain for the landing operation, who was also a carpenter and cabinet-maker. There was no hotel nor any craftsmen: tailors, shoemakers, bakers etc etc; there were thirteen white men and one female cook and housekeeper in the whole place.

For landing cargoes from steamers lying in the bay, the company had a short wooden jetty and owned a steam launch, two large lighters and several other boats. The protected bay did not have the same heavy surf as Swakopmund, but the almost constant strong south-westerly winds often caused a very choppy sea.

Once again, as in Walvis Bay, all cargo destined for the interior had to be carried by ox-waggon—except that transport was much more difficult through the long belt of sand dunes lying behind Lüderitzbucht, while the poor oxen had the last watering place at Tsirub after three days, and then on the return journey too often a seven day run without water. Watering an waggon-span oftwentyto 24 animals from the condenser was an expensive game; the water cost twenty marks per cubic metre, and I have often observed thirsty oxen drink 40 litres of water.

My predecessor, a sickly little man, was shot away by booze and head-over-heels in love with his housekeeper. At first I had a pretty hard time with the employees, over whom he had no authority, and who did exactly as they pleased. The engineer and the boatswain, especially, were devoted to drink, and believed themselves to be absolutely indispensible as nobody else knew anything about their work and replacements for them from Cape Town would take at the very least two months to arrive. It was not long before they were unashamedly playing up, and I did not spare their blushes. I sacked the engineer on the spot one day when I found him drunk at work, following repeated warnings. I banned him from entering the plant and I personally maintained the entire condenser system for two days.

The same thing happened a few days later with the boatswain. He had been drunk when a steamer arrived, and I had ended up steering the launch with two heavily-laden barges, bringing them safely from the steamer to land despite rough seas and strong winds. This had helped the two of them see that I would manage without them, and they timidly came back, apologised and asked for their jobs back. From then on we were good friends, and I never again had to complain about them. I had also explained to them that I fully understood them feeling the need to get drunk now and then in this otherwise godforsaken place… but never during working hours.

Lüderitzbucht was then a desolate spot. Apart from swimming and sometimes sailing in the bay it offered nothing, not a green blade of grass. During the summer months bare rock and sand, and constantly sharp winds from the southwest; in the winter often the terrible, scorching east wind.

In mid-1902 the Imperial Navy survey ship *Möwe* (*Gull*) came to Lüderitzbucht. As a representative of the Company and the coaling station I immediately made my calls to the commander and officers. These were officially returned on the same afternoon, and from then onwards, I enjoyed daily social contact with the ship's officers. The vessel carried out survey work on the coast every morning, coming back to the harbour at 6pm. Either the officers came to visit me on shore, or a boat brought me on board, and we were usually up till late, socialising. In fact, I was quite glad when the ship departed after six weeks, because although I was coping quite well, and all attempts by the officers to drink me under the table had failed, both my head and stomach were beginning to rebel against a surfeit of liquor.

The condenser system in place had to be enlarged, and a large steam boiler duly arrived from Hamburg. It had to be fitted without disrupting the condenser's operation or the water supply. All the equipment was stowed on board boats and barges, and could not be landed on shore, but the barges floated up to the shore on which the condenser station was built and the equipment hauled up the cliffs. A timber slipway was built on the cliffs, one of the side walls of the condenser station removed, and with much effort we succeeded in getting the new boiler to the right location to upgrade the condenser. Together with a mechanic from the steamship *Leutwein*, and drawing on my knowledge acquired from the old worsted spinning machine, we took four weeks to install the boiler and connect it to the old system.

There was no doctor or medical assistant in the settlement, and I played doctor, nurse and veterinary surgeon. For this I had ordered from Germany immediately after my arrival in Lüderitzbucht a wide selection of medicines, bandages and surgical instruments. I mended a Hottentot's leg fracture, and pulled a young settler woman's tooth without anaesthetic gas or painkilling injection.

In Kubub, about one hundred kilometres east of Lüderitzbucht we had a store and cattle posts, represented by Herr Klinghard, a kind old gentleman. Business affairs and negotiations with the district office necessitated a trip to Bethanien and Keetmanshoop. I was allowed three horses to Kubub, and rode on 30 September 1902 with a native boy and a packhorse with saddle, and arrived in Kubub on 1 October. There I was occupied for three days, and on 4 October left with fresh horses to continue my journey. Neither the boy nor I were paying attention overnight, and at daybreak we discovered that our horses had run away. It wasn't until the afternoon that the boy brought them back, finding them far from the camp. We rode the offenders hard for the next six hours, ensuring that they wouldn't run away next time.

Ubabis and Numis were within a day's ride, and after a morning on horseback I went for lunch on 7 October on the Sinclair Mine. At that time it was being worked by the engineers Cronin and Hampton for the firm A. Görz & Co., Johannesburg, and was leased from our Company. With Mr Hampton I spent two days going over the whole place: riding over to see the other copper deposits and several farmers and business customers of the Company from Goas to Chamis, where we arrived on 10 October. Hampton rode from there back to the mine, while I continued my journey and arrived on the morning of 11 October in Bethanien. There I had three pleasant days to recover, staying with the station chief *Leutnant* Baron von Stempel, who had offered on his visits to Lüderitzbucht to put up me and my horses; his victuals put the latter into very high spirits.

On 14 October I rode on to Kosis, trying to take a detour to shorten the route and leading the horses on a climb over high mountains. After riding some more, and having failed to find water during the day, we spent the night in an unknown riverbed. The next morning we followed the compass and finally came on to Kaxmas. After filling our water bottles and bellies with water, we went on by way of the Fish River to the Slangkop. There we stayed the night and arrived in Keetmanshoop on 16 October. I stayed there with the Burmester family, who had spent about ten days with me in Lüderitzbucht on their return from Germany in August, and now accommodated me with enormous kindness. It took several days to complete my business matters and official tasks; I was often in the officer's mess, and even spent pleasant days with the local medical officer and missionary.

On 21 October I began the return journey, over the Slangkop, Fish River and Neiams, along the Kuibis River, over the Kuibis and on 25 October to Kubub where I met *Leutnant* Ritter. [20] On the 26 and 27 October I was in Kubub, and with Klinghard rode across the whole area to find a suitable new place for our new cattle post until we selected Aus

---

[20] Hermann Ritter (b. 1873).

as the most appropriate spot, being both uninhabited and also having the only water source.

On 20 October I rode off with *Leutnant* Ritter along the route of the new railway planned by the government, always travelling cross-country without path or road. On 29 October we arrived back in Lüderitzbucht, where Ritter stayed with me for the next eight days. The journey was a total of 1,100 kilometres, and was both difficult and exhausting. During the great drought there was almost never enough pasture available in the bush for horses, and often you use a pack saddle to carry along oats and sacks with grass, when by good fortune you could get it. And the costs of transporting food by ox-waggon were enormous: thirty marks per 100lbs. In Keetmanshoop I had to pay 125 marks for a 140lb sack of oats.

In 1903 Dr Rhode stood down from the Company Board, and his place was taken by Herr von Bennigsen,[21] former governor of New Guinea. They decided in Berlin to convert the Lüderitz branch into a separate company, going into partnership with Herr Ludwig Scholz, who had been in Cameroon for years, and the Lüderitzbucht L Scholz & Co Company was founded (75% *DKG*, 25% Scholz).

I only learned about this in February 1903, when Herr von Bennigsen and Herr Scholz arrived in Lüderitzbucht and told me that Herr Scholz was taking charge of the new company. I had a thoroughly-deserved six months' leave to Germany and should then be transferred to Swakopmund. The leave with full pay and first class travel was very much to my taste, so naturally I didn't cause any headaches.

We had six weeks' strenuous work carrying out a full stock take, with Scholz naturally going by the valuation and I trying to represent the company's interests. I had to show Scholz all the operations of the business, and then finally during the second half of March 1903 I said goodbye to Lüderitzbucht and took the steamship *Hans Wörmann*, under my old friend Captain Becher, returning to my German homeland after eight years away in Africa.

---

[21] Rudolf von Bennigsen (1859-1912).

The journey was interesting and enjoyable, with the ship travelling along the entire West Coast, up through the Congo, Cameroon, Togo, Gold Coast, Liberia, Fernando Po etc. I landed in each of the ports with Captain Becher in the launch, visiting the country and going to the warehouses inland to collect cargo. After a journey of four and a half weeks we arrived in Hamburg, where I spent three days of big-city life before going by rail to my parents in Tetschen. I spent my leave there, enjoying Dresden, Berlin, Prague, Leipzig and Hamburg, and (as anyone can probably imagine) I did not miss out any of the pleasures and amusements that I had been away from for so long.

I cured my malaria, which I had in the blood, and my rheumatism, which I had in the bones, through a four-day cure at Teplitz.[22] While I was on leave my younger brother Ernst celebrated his wedding. All the beautiful girls in Tetschen were friends of his bride, and as an "old Africa hand" I had a good time, since I was considered to be a good catch. The mother of one of the nicest young women frequently invited me to their house, but I soon became suspicious when they began suggesting that it was probably time for me to get married. I explained that I was still too young and carefree, and they gave me up as a hopeless case.

From the managers of the company in Berlin I heard that they were dissatisfied with their commercial general manager in Swakopmund, and had dismissed him, and that I was to take over things. The contract that I had for Lüderitzbucht was immediately renewed for Swakopmund. On 30 September 1903 I stepped on board the old steamer *Adolph Wörmann* again to depart for Swakopmund. We had a lovely dinner party at the captain's table and the trip was pleasant and peaceful; the North Sea and the Bay of Biscay were stormy and after Mossamedes we came across a storm with such heavy seas that we arrived two days late in Swakopmund on 29 October.

The Swakopmund branch had the biggest goods business in the country. Wholesale and retail sales, a bank department and management of the company's land and mineral rights, with each

---

[22] Teplice, a spa town in the Czech Republic

department under a general manager. As our department measured the plots and farms sold by the company, the general manager and surveyor R. Schettler were constantly out working with two or three other surveyors. Lots of new work began for me; the department had to be reorganised because my predecessor in the credit business had guaranteed absurdly high credit in respect of the traders and farmers; I had to liquidate the business and pursue a number of new plans for the company. As always when a new manager competes for a position, he meets with some resistance from the staff who were sympathetic to his predecessor. I had to learn that this was especially the case with the manager of the Banking department, which included the accounting of goods received. I left it however to be proved by a trial of ability, and eased him out. He treacherously tried to blacken the character of myself and Schettler behind our backs, however Berlin took our side and he was dismissed. In November 1903 the Bondelswarts Hottentots rose up in the south of the country; this brought great upheaval and uncertainty to the country, and in January 1904 the Herero rose in revolt.

The Herero Rebellion 1904

Nachdem Se. Königliche Majeſtät von Sachſen etc.etc.etc.

den Vizefeldwebel im Landwehr-Bezirk I Dresden

Eugen Mansfeld

in Anſehung deſſen Allerhöchſtdenenſelben angerühmten guten Eigenſchaften ſeitigen Zwecks

zum Leutnant der Landwehr-Infanterie

in Gnaden ernennt und dermaßen beſtellt haben, daß Allerhöchſtdenenſelben er noch ferner getreu und dienſtgewärtig ſein, Seiner Königlichen Majeſtät und Höchſtdero Königlichen Hauſes Ehre, Nutzen und From-
men beſtmöglichſt befördern, Schaden und Nachteil aber, ſoviel an ihm, abwenden und verhindern, bei allen Vorfällen, wozu er befehligt werden möchte, ſich nicht nur unverdroſſen, pünktlich und tapfer erzeigen, ſondern auch nach Gelegenheit für Seiner Königlichen Majeſtät Allerhöchſten Dienſt ſeines Blutes, Leibes und Lebens nicht ſchonen, nicht minder alles übrige, ſo einem würdigen, klugen und rechtſchaffenen Offizier, auch jedem treuen Diener gegen ſeinen Herrn von Ehre und Pflicht wegen zu tun eignet und gebühret, ſchuldigſt beobachten, dagegen aber den dieſem Charakter zukommenden Rang und die gebührenden Ehren-

The Herero Rebellion 1904

After the Bonsdelswarts Uprising broke out in November 1903, the whole *Schutztruppe* was brought together in the south. We had already received word of several battles, and the uprising seemed to be taking on greater dimensions when the reserve conscripts of the German forces were notified to be ready for an eventual mobilisation. Suddenly on 11 January 1904 a telegraphic message arrived from Windhoek to say that three to four thousand armed and mounted Hereros were at Okahandja, their intention was not yet known, but there was no doubt that they were assembled, and that quite a hostile attitude prevailed. In Swakopmund all available reservists were immediately mobilised; I got my call-up at nine in the morning and by the afternoon we were all in uniform, a total of sixty men under the command of *Oberleutnant* von Zülow. The next morning after we had received weapons and supplies, the company set off by rail into the interior to rousing cheers from the population. In the rush, the wrong ammunition had been taken, and we had to wait at the station until the correct .808 rifle cartridges were sent on. Five-and-a-half hours later we arrived at Jakalswater Station; food was kept ready, and by seven o'clock we steamed on.

13 January 1904

Arrived at three o'clock in the morning at Karibib, we heard that a revolt of the Hereros had actually broken out, last night general murder had already begun in the country. Dickmann and his wife[23] and two other settlers were killed in Okahandja, and the garrison at Okahandja besieged by the Hereros. Karibib is on alert; there are 70 men there fit for service, of whom we are taking 30. Officers' swords and rank badges are put away, everyone is armed only with rifle, ammunition and bayonets, a precaution we have always observed

---

[23] Adolf and Henriette Diekmann and their baby son are buried at the Rhenish Cemetery in Gross Barmen.

because the Hereros knew the badge exactly and always focus their fire first on the officers' badges. At seven in the morning we go again, collect the settlers who have arrived at individual stations, and send warnings to those people staying. At Johann-Albrechtshöhe (Otjimakoko) the force is split into three companies. I am in One Company, under *Oberveterinär* Rickmann,[24] who is at the same time commanding the squads in the second company. We found the nearest station, Wilhelmshöhe, already abandoned and completely plundered by the Hereros. We had split the train in a station, stopping about 500 metres before it. Our first train, which had two carriages, crept out and inspected the station and the surrounding terrain, and lay there as cover while the locomotives took on water. The nearest station, Okasise, was also destroyed. The stationmaster and his assistant were lying dead in front of the house; we buried the two corpses. At six o'clock in the evening we arrived at Waldau. There everything was in readiness for war. Fourteen men had arrived from Karibib the previous day to protect the station, and the station buildings were already as well barricaded as possible. The rocks lying close behind the station were occupied by Herero troops. We had to stay in Waldau that night because we expected an attack and had to make preparations to continue the journey. Waldau is just twenty-three kilometres from Okahandja. The telegraph to Okahandja and back to Karibib was destroyed. I brought my company of twenty men to stay in the machine shed; I set four pairs of guards to keep watch, and twice during the night we were woken by the sentries shooting. At four in the morning the first enemy bullets whistled into the shed, and I ordered a quick withdrawal.

14 January 1904

Advancing at six o'clock on foot, One Company soon came on a Herero patrol which we finished off. After two hours' march we had to turn back, because we were suddenly fired on from behind, and it was

---

[24] Wilhelm Rickmann (b. 1869). Rickmann came to Namibia as a government veterinary officer in 1898 and was decorated for his work to combat rinderpest. He retired due to ill-health in 1907 and returned to Germany.

dangerous for us to be cut off. Back along the track embankment and turning left to scan along the hills, we got back to Waldau at half-past ten. As it would not be easy to continue advancing without being attacked, it was decided to armour the train. Each waggon—simple, open cargo trucks with wooden sides—was provided with a stack of ten sheets of corrugated iron on the sides, and behind them sacks full of rice and flour. The stocks came from Waldau, we built them up to chest height, and behind this armour the men were positioned, half sitting on the left, half on the right to the direction of travel, ready to fire. The train consisted of three sections:

1. A vanguard, i.e. a double locomotive with armoured car and a waggon with rail repair materials.
2. The main train: a locomotive, four armoured waggons and two goods waggons.
3. The rear guard: consisting of a double locomotive.

All three sections went along with fifty to sixty metres distance between each one. I was in the second waggon of the main train with my company of sixteen men. Building this train took all afternoon to complete, and was frequently interrupted when our sentries took heavy fire from the enemy, and we had to provide reinforcements. Towards evening, when the firing from the hills became intense, my train moved in front of the rocks and was able to shoot several Hereros. At night each section slept next to their waggon, and although we were roused several times, the Hereros did not dare to mount a proper attack.

15 January 1904
At 5.30am we set the trains moving. In less than half an hour we had a train crash, the rear guard locomotive drove into the main train, overturning the last carriage, which contained only kaffirs from Waldau (Waldau of course was evacuated), and derailed the baggage car into the middle of the tracks. We had an hour of hard work using winches to raise the car back onto the rails, the last waggon had simply been unhooked and thrown from the track. We went on with great care,

because from here on the track had been destroyed in many places; short lengths of rail ripped out and dragged away, railway cuttings blown up, and all these obstacles had to be cleared again. For this reason our One Company troops immediately swarmed out to the left and right and provided cover, and we were able to rout a much larger Herero patrol in Okakango. About twenty minutes before Okahandja was one final, much more extensive patch where the tracks had been destroyed and required repair. As soon as the train stopped we came under heavy fire from both sides of the railway tracks.

As always I jumped out with my company, on the left hand side, and we were barely ready to aim before we sustained a murderous barrage of shooting. As we were in open country, we had to traverse about sixty metres before we found cover in the trees. The black devils of the Okahandja field force came towards us in tight groups, and were stopped by a few well-aimed volleys that I directed. They carried on advancing, however they shot over our heads, wasting their ammunition. When the repairs to the track were finished, and we had to move back to the train, this was only possible by each man retreating backwards under covering fire from the right and left flanks, until we got back to the train. We carried on under covering fire from the waggons, getting to Okahandja at about 11.30am. The station was empty, occupied by neither us nor the Hereros—not by us because there was not enough manpower in the garrison to control it. The latter was lucky for us, since we would not otherwise have been able to remain at the station, and to storm it would have cost us heavy losses. As soon as the train stopped, some of the teams went out of the station building, while we occupied the embankment to the right of the tracks with two trains, and returned fire against droves of invading Herero. The enemy's fire was always heavy, and came at us from all four directions; but we gradually worked our way up the embankment by leaps and bounds until we were at the same height as Okahandja Fort.

After preliminary rapid fire and two salvoes came the command "Everyone to the fort, quickly!" Man after man, we had about one hundred metres to cover, over entirely open, clear terrain with bullets flying like a swarm of locusts. The main gate was barricaded, we had to dive through a narrow side gate, which was barricaded up to chest height, and two soldiers inside the gate pulled each man inside. During this entry we lost three men killed and two wounded. Okahandja Fort is a square building built of mud bricks, about sixty metres square, with a tower at each corner and designed to be easily defended. The fort had been besieged for three days; there were about one hundred people, men, women and children in it, and of course there was great joy because without our reinforcements of 120 men the garrison itself would not have been able to hold out much longer, especially since the command of the former *Distriktschef* and *Oberleutnant*[25] was questionable. This was not a sudden uprising: is proved by the simple fact that the very same night, from 12 to 13 January, farms were attacked everywhere in the country and the owners murdered. The rebellion was planned and organised for months, and so secretly that no whites, not even the missionaries, suspected anything. Okahandja looked devastated, all the private houses and stores looted and partly burned. A number of residents were murdered, and those who escaped to the fort owned only what they wore.

Now a terrible life began; a mass of people crammed together, while rain fell continuously day and night, so that mud stood a foot deep in the courtyard of the fort. The pump in the fort gave only a grey, muddy liquid that was unsuitable for consumption, and all available containers were prepared to collect rain for drinking water. *Oberleutnant* von Zülow[26] immediately took over command of the fort. The whole group was immediately allocated into three garrison companies and three field companies, the latter as an expeditionary corps which was set up to undertake sorties from the fort and attacks on the enemy. I was in One Field Company under our previous commander, *Oberveterinär* Rickmann, and commanded Two Section. I and my twenty men had one room as quarters; we were man to man next to one another on the stone floor, with only one blanket each, and for the first ten days did not take off our uniforms or boots. All the rooms were infested with bed-

---

[25] *Oberleutnant* Ralf Zürn
[26] Theodor Kurt Hartwig von Zülow

bugs, so that you were attacked by the delightful creatures, and even if you pulled one off there was another to take its place. Food was cooked in a large kitchen and each man collected it in his field mess-tin. Existing stocks were very scarce and not adequate for about two hundred people; the menu was very varied: rice, beans, peas and flour made from dried peas. Fresh meat did not exist; except in the first few days when we shot a couple of pigs which were still running around as well as an ancient, emaciated horse which was too unappealing even for the Hereros. The last of the pigs was especially tasty, because it was shot just as it was devouring the corpse of one of the Hereros who had been dead for several days.

The shooting went on day and night; the guard towers and embrasures were constantly double-manned. Every other day our section was on guard duty; and even though I did not have to stand guard myself I still had to inspect the positions, arrange the detachments and monitor all the operations. Anyone who was not on guard duty had work to do: the courtyard had to be drained, ditches dug, and windows and towers reinforced etc etc.

17 January 1904

On 17 and 18 January I had my section of the armoured train dismantled. We used the sacks to build a new redoubt, always under enemy fire. On 17 January I met Frau Lange, from Klein-Barmen, with two children. Her husband had been beaten to death by the Hereros before her eyes, and she received four blows to the head from a club and was left for dead. When she regained consciousness she was with the two children, girls of four and five years. They had escaped from the house into the bush and the Hereros did not find them; it took them five days to get to Okahandja, travelling only at night, barefoot and only partly dressed. All three were half-starved and in a terrible state, and we immediately took them into our care. Frau Lang's third child, a little girl of just over two years, was also beaten with a club by the Hereros. They thought she was dead, but an old Herero woman who had been one of the Lang's servants found the little girl sitting on her father's corpse and brought her to a missionary in Barmen, where a patrol later found her.

18 January 1904

At night, when I was at one of the turrets inspecting the guard, I heard movements outside the main gates and a voice called out, "Open up, open up."

"Who is there?" I called down.

"Meester Schulze," came the reply.

"I reckon I do know you," I shouted back, grabbed my rifle, and I and the turret crew opened heavy fire on Mr Schulze. The next morning we found six Hereros shot dead, lying in front of the gate, and the footprints of at least another twelve men. It appeared to be an enemy party trying to get into the fort.

19 January 1904

The three field companies went by armoured train in the direction of Osona, lying south of Windhoek, to explore whether and how far an advance was possible, and whether the railway line to Windhoek was destroyed. About a kilometre from the fort we came under heavy fire from the rocks to the right of the railway line; there, on top of a little hill, rings of small rocks. It was therefore an ideal defensive position. The house of the Herero headman, Barnabas, was there, and the previous day we had suffered heavy gun fire from there. Shortly before the train stopped there I was ordered by my commander to attack and capture the house. We stormed the house with bayonets fixed, the Hereros fled through the rear, and I deployed my men in the hillocks around the house. The train went on; I was to hold the ground overnight until it returned the next morning. The location was very good; we were indeed fired upon furiously from the hills lying opposite, but the position was such that with my sixteen men I could have lasted very well against an enemy force of two hundred rushing against us. The pleasure did not last long: after two hours the train returned, as the tracks had been destroyed so that travel any further was impossible.

20 January 1904

We had contact with neither Windhoek nor Swakopmund because the telegraph wires were destroyed. In order to get information about our fate and to find out more about conditions further down the line, a group of forty men under two reserve officers was sent by armoured train to break through in the direction of Karibib. The group went as far as Kawaturasane; there they came under fire from a superior Herero force, so that they had to retreat with the loss of four dead and four seriously wounded.

21 January 1904

Since this expedition was unsuccessful, but it was necessary for us to get despatches to Karibib, in the evening two Bergdamas (officers' servants) were cajoled and persuaded to make their way there on foot. These fellows sneaked by very smoothly and arrived in Karibib after four days, thereby relaying the first news of our fate to Swakopmund.

22 January 1904

We were busy fortifying another house (Gelhar)[27] near the station, to store a train there. About 4am we heard from the direction of Windhoek the repeated thundering of guns, and suspected the arrival of reinforcements. Work stopped immediately and after quarter of an hour the first two field companies moved out to occupy outposts on the hills overlooking the routes out of Okahandja to cover the advancing troops. In the pouring rain, under constant fire, we marched up to the Barnabas house to reoccupy it, with some of the soldiers going to the home of Paramount Chief Samuel Maherero[28] on the other side of the railway line. I and my team advanced two kilometres further to a rocky ridge from where I was able to cover the river crossing. Since the

---

[27] This was probably the Railway Hotel, whose proprietor was Fritz Gelhar.

[28] Chief of the Herero people of Okahandja, and leader of the Herero Rebellion. Following the end of the conflict he went to Bechuanaland (now Botswana) where he died in 1923. He is a Namibian national hero.

reinforcements failed to appear, we retreated back to the fort again under cover of darkness.

23 January 1904

We moved early at 7.30am with three columns in the same direction, but advanced several kilometres further, to the high Barmen hills that are just opposite the large bridge lying over the Swakop River. There a company of Hereros, about sixty men, mounted and on foot, wanted to draw us over the river; they came under heavy fire from us and fled, leaving many dead. Suddenly from the right and from the hills behind us we came under such fire that we could hardly find cover, and when the enemy watching us received numerous reinforcements we had to withdraw again.

25 and 26 January 1904

Work duty for the occupation troops and a half-day off for the expedition corps. We spent it in the fort's gardens, and requisitioned potatoes, vegetables and some magnificent grapes from the gardens of the company Wecke & Voigt, located on the Swakop River.

27 January 1904

The Emperor's birthday.

A field service was scheduled for 10am, where the missionary was to preach a sermon. At 8am we heard gunfire nearby again, and as we made the column ready to depart the Second Field Company under *Hauptmann* Franke[29] came up at the gallop, with a field gun and a mountain gun. We showed the guns off before the service, opening heavy fire on Kaiser Wilhelm Berg and the adjacent high ground, which lasted until 9am. At ten o'clock the missionary (who was nicknamed 'the holy eunuch' by the troops) arrived, but was quickly sent back home; because now we were celebrating the Emperor's birthday in a different way.

---

[29] Victor Franke (1865-1936). Franke was the last commander of the *Schutztruppe* in German South-West Africa, surrendering to South African troops in 1915.

As I already mentioned, the entire *Schutztruppe* was mobilised for the fight against Bondelswarts in the south, and on the news of the outbreak of the Herero uprising *Hauptmann* Franke was immediately ordered with his company to turn back and stay at Omaruru.

Here I would like to record something about the attitude of the missionaries, and especially the ones of the Rhenish Mission in Barmen. The missionaries played a singular role during the uprising: they remained sitting quietly in their houses, with Hereros going in and out. In Okahandja we came under the heaviest Herero fire from the church and the surrounding walled cemetery next to the missionary's house. His cows grazed outside, and when one of his living milk bottles was shot (our little children had no milk during all these festivities) the old man came running under the white flag of truce and wanted to make a huge fuss about it, but was turned away rather abruptly by our commanders.

Another day he came with a message from Samuel Maherero: give up all our women and children, and he would convey them to Swakopmund. We asked him if he was in his right mind, and gave him an answer. He and Samuel Mahahero were in it together as thick as thieves. In Otjisazu, two white settlers fled to the missionary's house; that day he told a gang of Hereros who had followed the pair that he did not know whether they were in his house or in the garden. The missionary left the front door open; the Hereros went inside, pulled out the two poor settlers and slaughtered them.

There is more to tell of these men, and the following little episode illustrates the rage and mood they provoked among the settlers: when I had to instruct my sentries in the lookouts about the different places in the town in the first days, I said to one old territorial soldier, "There is the mission house; you can only fire at it if someone shoots from it." He noticed the word 'if', and added "if the old bastard pokes his head out."

The Catholic priests on the other hand proved to be very different; they immediately put themselves at the disposal of the troops, and some even rode with the vanguard.

But enough of the holy spirits.

50

27 January 1904

After Franke's company joined us we heard that a train from Windhoek carrying provisions and ammunition was standing at the bridge at Swakop, the bridge had been destroyed at both ends. A division of our railway staff was immediately sent to repair the bridge, and we followed with two trains in order to provide cover to the workers.

28 January 1904

Hauptmann Franke and his company and the two guns set off early for Kaiser Wilhelm Berg and had a heavy battle against a much larger force of the Hereros, lasting many hours; the Hereros were decisively beaten. We were on the bridge all day again under fairly intense gunfire.

Two days before we arrived there, a detachment of 30 men with a machine gun had tried to come to Okahandja. One kilometre before the location where the railway line was destroyed, the detachment came under heavy fire from the Hereros, leaving behind five dead (including *Leutnant* D.R. Boyssen[30]) and had to withdraw. We discovered these five bodies on our return in the morning, and I went back with six men at six o'clock in the evening before the unit returned to the fort, with instructions to bury the fallen men. It was a terrible job. The corpses of course had been completely stripped and robbed by the Hereros, as they always do; they had already lain for fourteen days in the rain and hot sun; they stank, and were so terribly decayed and partly eaten by jackals that four of my men passed out. Naturally, each body could only be lifted with two spades, and was placed in a grave dug next to where the corpse lay.

---

[30] *Leutnant der Reserve* Raimund Boysen, who had settled in the colony with his parents. The other dead soldiers were *Unteroffizier* Päch, *Gefreiters* August Rudolph and Josef Zülot, and *Reiter* Wilhelm Gerwinsky.

29 January 1904

After *Hauptmann* Franke had defeated the Hereros at Kaiser Wilhelm Berg the day before, we now began looking for the enemy on the other side of the mountain. At six in the morning, 85 men under the command of *Leutnant* von Zülow marched out, climbed the high mountain and the adjoining hills, and met only scattered small groups of the enemy. Those Herero who were not shot, fled; and we concluded that the mountain and the surrounding area could be considered to have been evacuated by the enemy. The troops returned to the fort in the afternoon.

30 January 1904

Troops were allocated to the various railway stations to protect the railway line.

31 January 1904

Hauptmann Franke and his company and guns withdrew from Karibib to Omuaruru, which is besieged by the Hereros. At a battle in Osona, Franke's company lost a large number of horses to the Hereros. They took away and kept thirty animals, and let the remaining thirty-nine come back to us. Of these, the majority are currently unfit for use; they were in a miserable condition, with most of them bearing terrible, large, open pressure sores on their backs and withers. We managed to find twelve useable horses. I got a pretty, four-year-old, brown Afrikaner mare, which they probably only left to return back to the company because of her two faults: hard to catch and difficult to mount. I soon figured out catching her, and I was not bothered by her restlessness when mounting: I am always in the saddle. However, at the battle of Barmen these two vices would almost prove disastrous for me. Gradually we treated the rest of the horses, and soon our whole train was mounted. We were now the elite, justly envied by the others, but this also brought extra duties looking after the horses in the morning and evening.

3 February 1904

Early at five o'clock in the morning we made our first major patrol, from Okahandja via Okakango to the farm Otjisawakumbe, where we found the owner Utz and his wife murdered, and the farm ransacked, and once again we had to play gravedigger. On the way to Waldau we caught two Hereros armed with rifles, whom we simply hung on the next tree. Waldau was clear of the enemy, and as we encountered no further Hereros on searching the surrounding area, we started to ride back and were in Okahandja at seven o'clock that night.

4 February 1904

The first soldiers sent from Germany arrived in Okahandja; a troop of twenty men under *Oberleutnant* Winkler with a division of Marines, who travelled immediately to Windhoek.

4 February 1904

In the afternoon the Boer de Jager rode up, and reported that there were a lot of Boers with women, children and cattle on the farm Okambambe, together with a Frau Hoth with two children and the young Wecke[31] (son of the first merchants in Swakopmund), and that they were hard pressed by the Hereros. At 3 o'clock our platoon stood saddled-up in front of the fort, and after three-and-a-half hours hard ride we arrived in Okambambe. There were fifty-four people there altogether, a crowd of Boer women and children. Frau Hoth, whose husband was murdered, had a serious gunshot wound in the leg, and was immediately patched up by our doctor, *Stabsarzt* Dr Jacobs, who had joined the expedition. All were instructed immediately to pack their belongings and loaded onto their waggons and to get ready for departure. I was on guard until midnight, sentry posts all around the farm house, and could only dream of sleeping that night.

---

[31] Probably Claude Wecke, who was the son of Fredrick Christian Wecke, one of the founders of the Namibian department store Wecke & Voigts. Claude Wecke was almost eleven years old.

10 February 1904

At four in the morning we departed, and escorted the seven ox-waggons loaded with women and children and all their belongings; a bullock cart with the wounded Frau Hoth and her two children, as well as three large herds of cattle to Waldau, where we arrived at seven o' clock in the morning. We loaded the woman and children onto a train to be taken to Okahandja; we had riders accompany the waggons and cattle to Okahandja, and arrived there in the afternoon.

10 February 1904

Leutnant Griebel has been ordered back to Swakopmund and I have to take over his Two Company—to my great annoyance, as I wanted to stay with our detachment. *Oberleutnant* von Zülow also returns to Swakopmund as *Etappenkommandant*, and Reserve *Oberleutnant* Zürn[32] goes back as garrison commander, to everyone's chagrin.

12 February 1904

In the evening the mounted company rides for Barmen. I am not allowed to go with them as the *Seebateillon* (naval light infantry) should arrive tonight. Zürn was the only officer in the fort, and I was busy with my garrison company.After a fruitless night on watch, the train arrived with the *Seebateillon* and a detachment of marine artillery, forty men altogether, under *Major* von Glasenapp[33].

13 February 1904

Early up, at half-past five, and 150 men immediately set off riding towards Windhoek. I had already prepared their accomodation, so that all troops were soon billeted. At half-past-six in the evening the *Major* suddenly sounded the alarm for the entire garrison. My company

[32] Ralf Zürn was the *Distriktschef* in Okahandja. Samuel Maherero specifically named him as the main instigator of the conflict between the settlers and Hereros.
[33] Franz Georg von Glasenapp (1857-1914), later commander in chief of the German colonial forces.

was mustered in front of the fort ready to march off in less than ten minutes, long before the newly-arrived troops, for which he gave us a special commendation.

14 February 1904

On Sunday I accompanied *Major* Glasenapp and two officers who had not sat on a horse for a long time, and who wanted to see something of the destruction of the farms, on a ride to Okakango and back.

At five-thirty in the afternoon our riders came back from Barmen. Between Gross-Barmen and Klein-Barmen they came under such fire from a superior force of Hereros that they were forced to retreat, without being able to complete their mission. The latter consisted of a detachment of sailors from the cruiser *Habicht* (Hawk) and a new *Schutztruppe* company, in Barmen under the command of *Kapitänleutnant* Gygas,[34] and expected to keep the place clear of the enemy. Glasenapp, dissatisfied, ordered the immediate return of the mounted detachment and to keep Barmen at all costs. At the request of Glasenapp I was relieved as commanding officer of the garrison company and reassigned to the mounted division again, much to the fury of Zürn, who could not understand that I did not want to remain in a safe and harmless post in the fort.

We chose a different route this time. One *Seebateillon* company under *Hauptmann* Liber, and an ox-waggon with provisions and ammunition for the troops accompanied us. The infantry marched at half-past seven in the morning, and we followed at eight; at ten o'clock we passed them, riding onwards to the farm Okatjirude and arriving at eleven. Two hours later the infantry joined us there, and all remained there for the night.

---

[34] Hans Gygas (1872-1963); the First Officer of *Habicht*, which had put in for repairs at Cape Town. When the rebellion began, the ship was ordered to Swakopmund and Gygas put in charge of a force to help fight the Herero. Gygas saw active service in the First World War and retired in 1919 with the rank of *Konteradmiral*.

15 February 1904

Rose at five o'clock and moved off. We rode as an advance party about five to six hundred metres ahead, past Otjisaru to Okamarusu where we waited for the ground forces. I rode with two men about three kilometres along the river to look for a watering hole, but had to return back empty-handed; and since there was no water at Okamarusu, the entire company had to return to Otjisaru. We met there at midday and dismounted for a lunch break. The watering hole was a vlei about 40 metres in diameter and about a metre deep. To begin with, we fished out a dead ox and a dead Herero from the water. It looked uninviting; apart from being the colour of cocoa, nobody knew if it had been poisoned by the Hereros. First of all we made the weakest horse and one of our own natives drink it; when neither of these two dropped down dead, we let ourselves taste the dark broth. It did quench our thirst, but it took ages.

Here Liber's company eventually fulfilled their objective by means of acquiring some Herero cattle, and returned to Okahandja with their ox-waggon at five o'clock in the morning. We rode from half-past five (*Oberleutnant* von Dobeneck from the detachment joined us) from Okamarusu until just before Barmen, near the so-called Schlangenkoppe where we unsaddled and in total silence, without making a fire, spent the night.

16 February 1904

At five o'clock in the morning we rode off, taking the utmost precautions, because we faced a ride which went through a particularly unfriendly pass. We were very close to Barmen and expected to find the place full of Hereros. By half past seven we were in Barmen. One section rode immediately to the fort; the first company under Rickman searched the houses and the river valley, and I had the second company inspect the church, mission house and the native houses. There were no Hereros. In one native home we found a newborn lamb; straight into the house, knife out, throat cut, it only took a moment. In the next house we found four chickens; we wrung their necks just as quickly, and then rode proudly to the fort, with our looted foodstuffs. We had something to eat for the time being, at least; we each had nothing in our knapsacks other than two hard ship's biscuits and a piece of bacon, and nobody knew how long we would be staying in our new palace. The military fort had been totally destroyed by the Hereros, they had smashed the walls for the most part, turning it into a giant pile of rubble, and the building was uninhabitable. Since Barmen seemed to be empty of Hereros, we pitched our camp outdoors. From midday to five o'clock I had four-man outposts set on the highest hills in Barmen, about two kilometres away from the fort; they saw no Hereros.

The interior of the mission house was also destroyed, we found in among the rubble all sorts of things we could use: cooking utensils, plates, spoons and knives, and in the garden there were even vegetables and fresh maize for us to take.

17 February 1904

At seven o'clock in the morning I went back to the mission house. First I shot a chicken that ran across the road towards me and then, with six men, I set all the native houses alight. The black rascals had all their belongings piled up in the church, packed in boxes and suitcases. All were opened up with an axe and carefully searched; collected together in front of the church; doused with paraffin, and then we had a nice little bonfire. At ten o'clock a patrol under *Oberleutnant* Paaschen[35] and Reserve *Leutnant* Oswald came from Okahandja with an ox-cart, along with an eight-man escort, to bring us provisions and oats for our horses. I had acquired some fresh maize cobs in the mission, which we roasted among the ashes. Together with curried chicken and rice, we entertained our guests royally. In the afternoon the two newly-arrived officers and I wandered around the mission house again, finding all sorts of useful things and vegetables and maize in the garden, and finally I was able to shoot a nice cockerel that had nervously hidden itself in a tree. With everything stowed in a hand basket, we were on the way back when suddenly shots rang out from the hill behind the mission

[35] Probably *Oberleutnant* Paschen of the Marine Infantry.

house, one of which landed between me and Oswald. We had a good twenty-minute walk to the fort across totally open terrain: rocky, uphill, and without any cover. Oswald called to me to throw my bag away because I could run better, but there was nothing more I could do, so I wasn't going to give up my cockerel to the Hereros. We straight away brought the horses, carts and oxen to the kraal behind the fort; and, lying under cover of the rubble of the fort, we immediately returned fire until darkness fell and the Hereros stopped shooting. Sleeping within the walls was practically impossible, as the wreckage on which we were lying almost broke our backs.

18 February 1904

By five o'clock in the morning I had had enough; I sat down, and at the very moment I had lit my pipe, and was thinking about my mother in Tetschen, the other side began shooting. At first I was delighted, and even waved my thanks to the rocks opposite because I thought the Hereros were so considerate to have organised a gun salute to mark my mother's birthday, but as an 88er bullet[36] struck the ground about a metre in front of me, I realised that the gentlemen meant it for me. Our side returned vigorous fire at once; but we could not move out from the wreckage of the fort, and at ten o'clock the enemy ceased firing and moved off.

19 February 1904

At four in the morning the patrol moved off with the ox cart to return to Okahandja, we had to carry on waiting here.

At half-past eight a ten-strong mounted patrol came, under *Oberleutnant* Ritter, the head of the Otjimbingwe detachment we had been waiting for (very jolly). He said that they had not seen a single Herero between Klein- and Gross-Barmen. We were puzzled, because we had observed Hereros in the hills just a short while before. The detachment was due to arrive in about two hours and, to protect them from surprises, we decided to ride to Klein-Barmen with Ritter's patrol.

---

[36] The 8.08mm bullet fired by the *Gewehr* 88 German army rifle.

We set off at half-past nine, twenty-eight riders, with one sergeant and eight men remaining as a guard. After a short ride we came to the home of the farmer Rosenthal,[37] completely destroyed. We found Rosenthal lying murdered in the cattle kraal, and buried what remained of him in a grave which we scraped out with our hands, as we lacked a spade. In the meantime Feldwebel Säring had been sent with six men to scout to the left around the cliffs located there; when he did not return, we rode to the cliffs at a full gallop in *Schützenlinie* (skirmish-line) formation. Suddenly, two hundred metres ahead of us, a bunch of Hereros jumped out of the rocks and opened fire on us. We rode to the left, brought our horses into cover, leaped off and took up the fight. We had the enemy under heavy fire and were about to storm their positions, when... Boom! Suddenly an artillery grenade whizzed over our heads. Shortly afterwards, shrapnel burst a short way behind us, and at the same moment a second grenade exploded near us. "Everyone to the horses! Get out and gallop back on whatever you can ride, our own artillery are firing at us!"

What had happened was this: *Kapitänleutnant* Gygas had just arrived on the scene with sixty crewmen from the *Habicht*, and fifty new *Schutztruppe* troops and two guns from Otjimbingwe (the advance party under *Oberleutnant* Ritter was already with us). The cliffs that we were about to storm lay between him and us, and since he was engaging with enemy in the cliffs, he opened fire on them with his guns. We rode back until we were out of range of the guns, with two horses shot, and occupied the left-hand-side of the path leading up, in order to cut off the enemy's retreat. With six men, I went further forward and occupied a hill at the enemy's flank. The fight lasted six hours until the enemy was displaced from his position and all the rest of them retreated back in a stampede. Once our troops had withdrawn, Gygas directed us for deployment to Barmen. We followed everyone else, providing cover at the rear of the column, and arrived at the fort at five o'clock in the afternoon, tired, hungry and thirsty.

---

[37] Probably Otto Rosenthal, whose grave at Gross Barmen states that he was killed on 12 January 1904.

We were looking forward to a rest, but did not get one, because there were nine men seriously wounded (one man missing, believed killed) who needed to be brought overnight with a mounted escort to Okahandja. We just had time to feed and water our horses and grab a bite to eat ourselves, and at six-thirty the detachment stood saddled-up and ready to move off again. Sixteen troops rode ahead with Gygas and *Oberleutnant* Ritter, then an ox-cart with the wounded, and ten riders and myself providing an escort at the rear. It was a dismal journey, because the ox-cart drove very slowly over the bad roads; we had to keep to its pace, and so we finally arrived in Okahandja at two in the morning.

Eight hours on horseback at walking speed after spending the entire day in the saddle and fighting, you can only imagine what the riders went through. I prefer four hours trotting and cantering to an hour at walking pace. In order to provide relief during the slow progress, every now and then I permitted men to dismount and lead their horses. The waggon constantly enveloped us in a cloud of dust, and occasionally we halted and allowed it to proceed forward for some distance, so that at least we had the opportunity to trot a short way. At one point during these manoeuvres the waggon got about 200 metres ahead of us. As we trotted to catch it up, *Kapitänleutnant* Gygas was there in the middle of the road, and he tore me off a strip: I was supposed to be escorting the waggon, not going out for a nice canter in the country. Since he refused to accept the explanation I gave him for my actions, I angrily gave the command "Dismount! Lead horses!" Gygas gave me a disapproving look and rode back to the front.

In Barmen our quarters were occupied, so we dismounted in front of the fort and spent the night sleeping on our saddles. I was up early, and met *Kapitänleutnant* Gygas. He immediately stopped me and said "Was it you leading the patrol behind the cart with the wounded? You're a fine chap: first I reprimand you, and then you give the order, 'Dismount!' You actually meant 'Kiss my arse,' didn't you?"

I did not say anything, but when he asked again, I replied "If that's what the Herr *Kapitänleutnant* thinks, then I have to agree."

Gygas laughed, shook hands and took me inside the fort for a large glass of schnapps.

24 February 1904

We had received news that there were Hereros settled with cattle at Okamita, about twenty-five kilometres north of Okahandja, and orders came for an expedition. At eleven o'clock at night we set off; thirty mounted riders at the front, then two guns and a *Seebataillon* company on foot under *Hauptmann* Scheering. We stopped from one till three, and let the horses graze with their saddles on; it was a cold night and none of us were thinking of sleep.

25 February 1904

At five in the morning we arrived at Okamita, a large Herero village in a beautiful location, with good pasture and water. The guns were hauled to the top of a hill, and we horsemen galloped in *Schützenlinie* formation from the left towards the village before the infantry went in from the right. The village was deserted; after searching the surrounding area and confirming that none of the enemy could be found, we set the huts on fire. Our task was fulfilled; Scheering's section remained in place until the afternoon, while the mounted troops started back after an hour's rest. We found on the road the bodies of *Feldwebel* Kühnel and a trooper who had been missing since the outbreak of the uprising; in other words, they had died there while out on patrol.

26 February 1904

The telephone line to Windhoek stopped working and needed to be repaired by *Feldpostsekretär* Thorun, and I had to ride with a patrol of four troopers to escort him. He soon found the damage, and on the way back we had a little race with the train coming from Windhoek... which we won handsomely.

27 February 1904.

At nine o'clock in the morning, I was sent by train to Windhoek with a special message from *Oberst* Dürr;[38] it was nice to do something different for a change. There were two days to wait until I could return, and the time passed pleasantly with invitations to see friends, as well as in the officer's casino. I was also able to attend the execution by hanging of four Hereros.

29 February 1904

In the morning I returned to Okahandja.

1st March 1904

I spent the morning with *Oberleutnant* Ritter and *Leutnant* Oswald. We were building targets for artillery halfway up Kaiser Wilhelm Berg. We held a shooting competition in the afternoon.

2 March 1904

A bigger expedition to the Kuiseb had been planned, it was anticipated that it would eventually last between two and three weeks. All preparations were made, and at seven o'clock in the evening we moved off. There were two mounted field companies leading the column, formed of fifty troopers under *Oberleutnant* Ritter, I was in charge of the first company, and the second was under the command of *Leutnant* Oswald. Next came four guns under *Leutnant* Samuelsen and *Leutnant* Rümann[39] then a *Seebataillon* company commanded by *Hauptmann* Scheering. and a new *Schutztruppe* company under *Hauptmann* Puder.[40] In total we were 250 men, with *Hauptmann* Puder

---

[38] Probably Karl Dürr, who was the commander of the marine units sent from Germany.

[39] Wilhelm Rümann (1881-1946). After a career in the German Navy in which he rose to the rank of *Konteradmiral*, Rümann joined the Nazi Party, becoming a *SS-Oberführer* and serving on Himmler's staff.

[40] Harry Puder (1862-1933). Puder spent much of his army career in the German colonies, with service in German East Africa, German South-West Africa and German Cameroon.

in overall command. About one hour's ride from Barmen we stopped and waited for the rest of the column, remaining there until dawn.

3 March 1904

At six in the morning the mounted troops rode at full gallop into Barmen and found it abandoned by the enemy. Two hours later the infantry arrived, with seven ox-waggons bearing provisions and ammunition, guns, a field ambulance and so on, and we decided to camp at the fort. At two o'clock that afternoon, *Oberltn.* Ritter, eight men and I were sent forward to Klein-Barmen for reconnaissance. We rode about twelve kilometres, checking out each cliff and mountain with the greatest caution, until we found fresh tracks of Herero and cattle at one location in the bed of a river. On foot, three of us explored the area until we could be entirely certain that we were very close to the enemy. We made our way back to Barmen, arriving at half-past seven, and spent the night making preparations to move off the next morning.

4 March 1904

We marched off at five in the morning, once more the mounted troops rode in front, with *Oberltn.* Ritter and me leading the detachment. We went ahead in absolute silence, but scouts reported that the cliffs from which we took such heavy fire on 19 February were empty. At Rosenthal's Farm we branched off to the left, riding straight across the river-bed, and began to ascend the steep hill on the other side until we joined the road to Okahandja. To the right of this road are tall mountains stretching out towards Klein-Barmen. It was here that the fight occurred on 19 February resulting in the loss of one of the marines. After searching for a while we found the remains of his body and covered it with large stones, as burial without a spade was impossible in the hard ground. Here I should point out that the Hereros always take the dead and rob the bodies straightaway. They usually mutilate them by cutting off the genitals. Those who are only wounded and cannot retreat are clubbed to death with knobkerries, a beastly death. If you happen to be wounded when on patrol or in a battle then, rather than fall into the hands of these animals, the usual idea is that you save the last bullet for yourself.

We took the route shown in the sketch below:

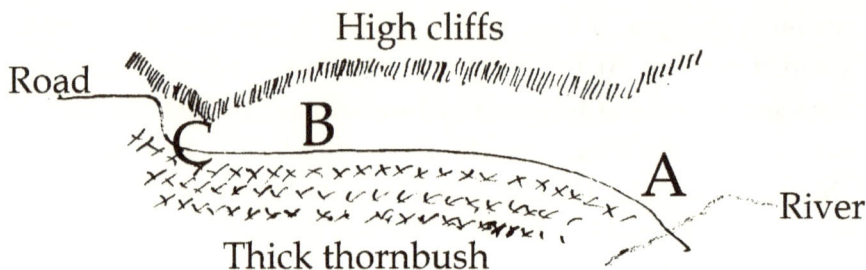

High cliffs

Road

C   B

A

Thick thornbush

River

Figure 2. Sketch plan of Klein Barmen 4 March 1904

At point A the road crossed over another small river, and on the right hand side the cliffs and mountains appeared closer and closer to the road.   At point B we stopped briefly and Ritter and I used binoculars to scan the high ground without seeing a trace of any Hereros. We carried on trotting slowly, observing acutely and listening to every sound, until we arrived at about point C, where the cliffs directly overlooked a bend in the road. Suddenly there was a 'Bang! Bang!' and two shots right into the middle of our column. My horse reared straight up, and I felt certain that it would be shot. For a moment everything was still, then I saw rifle after rifle blazing at us from out of the cliffs only about fifty metres away. A glance backwards showed that it was impossible for us to retreat, as we were also under fire from behind, and just then the black devils came running from the entire length of the mountains like a swarm of ants.

There was just one command: "To the left, and keep riding!" To the left of the road was dense thorn bush, strewn with loose stones and large rocks. We had neither seen nor anticipated that on the right we would be greeted by a line of Hereros shooting at us from a ledge. It was just a case of getting through and finding cover. Our situation was terrifying, and it is a miracle that so many of us escaped. The thick bush ripped away both of my stirrups, and I had one of the sleeves of my coat torn straight off. I lost my seating as we jumped over bushes and rocks; hanging down on the left side of the horse, and had to pull myself back up into the saddle by grabbing onto her mane. A riderless horse galloped alongside me; at exactly the same moment I grasped its reins, my own horse collapsed under me—fatally hit by a bullet. My luck in catching the second horse continued until finally we all gathered behind an outcrop about two metres in height and about ten metres long. Before I could dismount, my second horse crashed to the ground; so I had lost two horses shot under me in less than five minutes. Just then I got lucky when three more horses without riders trotted past on the loose, so I claimed my third horse of the morning. We immediately opened fire on the enemy.

When I counted my men I noticed with horror that of thirty of us, eighteen were missing: dead or taken cover, who could say? And then once again a dense firing-line of about one hundred Hereros approached from the right flank, shouting furiously at us. We were coming under fire from the left, and were thus blocked in on three sides. It was impossible for us to stay behind such sparse defences, so we mounted our horses again and galloped over the wide, unsheltered riverbed up to a small hill which lay on the opposite bank.

As we rode away the Hereros called after us in German, "You're out of luck now!" On the hilltop we found good cover for our horses in the dense bush; two men stayed to guard the horses, the rest of us arranged ourselves in a semicircle around the edge of the hill and immediately opened heavy fire on the enemy following us. For two hours we lay there, holding the enemy at bay until the first artillery shell crashed into the mountains and we knew that the main detachment had arrived. The two companies were coming to relieve us. We gained a breathing space, because the Hereros surrounding us retreated back to their comrades in the mountains. As the battle developed, the artillery pounded the high ground; as soon as the enemy moved positions he came under fire from our infantry, and must have suffered very heavy losses. They sent a gun up to join us, because we were in a good, commanding position, and Rickmann and *Stabsarzt* Dempwolff[41] also came to our position. Ritter was surprised to find me alive; one of our troopers, who had made his way back to the main column, reported that the leading troops had been killed in the ambush. In the meantime, another five of our riders were discovered on foot, their horses having been shot under them.

We had orders to occupy the hilltop, to cover the left flank of the enemy, and to gradually move down the hill to the riverbed. The Hereros also moved from peak to peak on the left, occupying the high ground opposite us. The battle lasted seven hours, to two o'clock in the afternoon, when the enemy retreated in headlong flight, and the infantry companies occupied the two highest peaks facing us.

Then came orders from *Hauptmann* Puder that we should ride towards the left and eventually break through the Herero forces and cut off their cattle. That was unfeasible, because we were only twelve men; and we still had to provide cover for the passage of the ox-waggons, as they would otherwise have fallen into Herero hands. I therefore had to convey an appropriate reply to Puder.

After a long search I finally tracked him down on top of a mountain with the infantry companies. After getting further orders I rode back. It was a long road, and it had been a good hour since I first rode along it. Ritter had gone further on with the other riders—devil knows where—and I was riding on my own opposite the hills occupied by the enemy. Suddenly two shots went right past my head. I leaped off the horse and responded to this greeting with a few shots of my own, then quickly jumped back on and cut across to the right at a gallop. I caught up with the seven ox-waggons at the river crossing. On the other side of the river I found five of our missing troopers; three joined me,

---

[41] Otto Dempwolff (1871-1938). After the Herero War, Dempwolff's field of professional interest shifted from medicine to linguistics. In 1918 he became professor at the University of Hamburg, where he was head of the Department of Indonesian and South Pacific languages.

and I left the two men who had no horses to ride in the ox-cart. After we had ridden about half an hour we met the field ambulance with two medical officers and some of our troopers; and *Oberleutn.* Ritter showed up at the same moment with the rest of our company. By counting and roll-call it was established that nobody knew anything of the fate of five of our troopers: *Unteroffizier* Valenziak, Saar, Zöllner, *Gefreiter* Mockita and *Reiter* Amft, were missing. Only *Unteroffz.* Saar had been reported as dead.[42] The infantry and guns were about half-an-hour's ride ahead of us. As the battle was now over, they had set up camp beside the water below a small hill.

In order to determine the fate of our five men, whether they were dead or wounded, we sixteen remaining riders were ordered to turn round and go back. We had to return to the trap, where we were first fired on. We rode back to the first hilltop we had occupied, left the horses tied up, and went with our rifles in our hands down to the site of the ambush. After an hour of searching we had found all five men— dead. All were stripped naked and mutilated. Four of them had died after being shot in the head; only poor Zöllner had been horribly singled-out: battered with knobkerries, mutilated, with one arm entirely torn off and laid across his body. I cannot describe how we felt. Our little mounted company of thirty men had paid the price today. Five men dead; two men wounded and fourteen horses killed. What was more, the other companies had had no men killed or injured.

After we had buried the dead as best we could, Ritter said a few words and a short prayer and we fired three volleys over the graves. We went quietly to the horses and rode silently to the encampment, where we arrived at five o'clock that afternoon.

5 March 1904

Early in the morning near the camp we liberated fifty head of small livestock and as many again of cattle, which in their desperate haste the Hereros had not been able to take with them. At three in the

---

[42] *Unteroffizier* Andr. Waleciak, Albert Saar and Hermann Zöllner, and *Reiter* Emil Mykitta are buried at the cemetery in Gross Barmen.

afternoon the expedition began to move off again, with our riders (now twenty men strong using the spare horses) at the forefront.

At a quick gallop we headed past Klein-Barmen to the farm Snyrivier, which turned out to be free of the enemy. Here again everything had been destroyed or looted. Behind the house we found the bodies of the owners,[43] murdered and mutilated by the black villains, and buried them. While awaiting the arrival of the remainder of the expedition, we constructed a kraal for the horses and trek oxen and put the water-pump back up in its place by the well. The entire column camped here.

6 March 1904

At four o'clock in the morning a patrol from Puder's company under *Leutnant* von Rosenberg went out to explore the area together with two Boers who knew the local area. The patrol came at back at eight o'clock with the news that a large group of Hereros with cattle was sitting south of the Swakop river.

To lead successful attack would have needed at least three times the troop strength, and it was therefore decided to leave the band undisturbed, and to strengthen Okahandja first. Staying and waiting any longer at Snyrivier was pointless because it would have wasted provisions, so it was agreed to move on to the railway line at Okasise. We left at two in the afternoon. The enemy was behind us, therefore we formed the column back-to-front, and Ritter and I rode last of the entire company. An hour later we were on Otjiruse, one of the most beautiful places in Hereroland, and a tenanted farm with beautiful pasture and good water. The horses and oxen drank, and four o'clock the column set off again.

Ritter and I fancied a schnapps, so we told the commissary, who was travelling in comfort on an oxcart, that we had had terrible stomach cramps, and managed to con him out of two bottles of rum before setting up camp for the night at seven o'clock.

---

[43] The brothers Hans and Herman Lange, who were killed on 12 January 1904 and are buried on the farm Klein-Barmen.

7 March 1904

We set out at five in the morning, but the column began to falter after a waggon overturned on the steep road. Once again we rode at the head of the column, and sped to Fahlwater at full gallop, arriving at ten o'clock. There was a government building there as well as a house and store belonging to the Talaska family, farmers. The houses were still there, but everything inside had been stolen; the owners had fled in time. It rained in the afternoon and evening, so I became sick. With terrible stomach cramps.

8 March 1904

At eight in the morning we arrived at Okasise. *Oberst* Leutwein was coming from Karibib and was expected within the hour. Then a message came from Okahandja to say that Chief Samuel Maherero was at Otjisazu with 4,000 Hereros.

When Leutwein arrived he was delighted to find us at Okasise, and ordered the immediate return of all troops to Okahandja. The foot soldiers were transported by railway; the ox-waggons would take two days' march to get to Okahandja, guarded by marching infantry on the way; while the troops on horseback were ordered to arrive in Okahandja that night. We set off at two o'clock, with ten mules pulling field guns following us. Soon after setting off there was a heavy storm, and a terrible downpour that lasted to Waldau, where we arrived at 5pm. We only stopped at Waldau to let the animals drink, and then we carried on at a sharp pace, so we were in Okahandja by nine that night.

Our quarters had already been occupied, and so, wet as we were, we had to spend the night on the open verandah of the fort, sleeping on our saddles. Luckily we were so tired that we slept well anyway. None of us had a dry stitch on our bodies; our riding boots had water inside, and the men's army boots were filled to the top with water. The journey from Fahlwater to Okasise to Okahandja is seventy-eight kilometers long, and in pouring rain it wasn't exactly a pleasure trip.

9 March 1904

In the morning there was a major reorganisation of the entire garrison and a march past in front of the governor, *Oberst* Leutwein.

As there were no more big military operations to be undertaken in the immediate future, and there were ample new troops from Germany available for disposal, the assembled reservists were discharged. For the time being I was allocated to the military supply headquarters at Swakopmund.

10 March 1904

I slowly made my way by train.

12 March 1904

I arrived in Swakopmund at eleven o'clock.

13 March 1904

In the morning I reported to *Oberleutnant* von Zülow at the military supply headquarters, where I served as Adjutant until my final release on 25 March.

Figure 3. The certificate for Mansfeld's South West Africa campaign medal.

After the Herero War

After the Herero War

After returning to Swakopmund I was drafted into the service of the garrison commander. For two months I had military duties each morning, but was free to pursue my job at the Company for the rest of the day. Business was booming in Swakopmund, and Rheede sometimes had as many as twenty steamers bringing troop transports, equipment and food from Germany; and oxen, horses, mules and food supplies from Cape Town.

With the transport of animals a lot of shady characters came from the Union,[44] and fights, robberies and shootings in the streets were soon so bad that one could no longer go out unarmed at night.

Even in my room, in the upper floors of the exhibition building, one such drunken individual came at night, when I was fast asleep, apparently with the intention of enquiring as to my well-being. As I wasn't used to such kindness, I leaped out of bed and sent him flying with a punch in the mouth and a kick in the belly, so that he fell backwards through the doorway and tumbled back down the full length of the staircase.

As the mole built in Swakopmund in 1901 began to silt up, it was no longer sufficient for the landing operation. As a result a German engineering company built, in a very short time, a wooden jetty extending two hundred metres into the sea.

In January 1904 Spitzkopje was overrun by the Hereros, who looted the farm and murdered the local manager. In mid-August 1904 I was to ride there to evaluate what remained. I was to go alone, accompanied only by a native. This was a bit risky, because since the scattered Hereros roamed around pretty much everywhere, I had to assume that they were safely entrenched among the fine pasture and ample water that Spitzkopje enjoyed, thanks to the plentiful rain that year.

---

[44] i.e. the British South African colonies

An opportunity arose, as Chief Engineer Tönnissen of the Otavi Mines and Railway Company had to go to Spitzkopje in order to make astronomical calculations. He persuaded the military headquarters to fit him out with a four-man military escort under the command of *Oberleutnant* Freiherr von Fritsch, together with a four-span mule cart. Tönnissen and I had superb horses, and the driver of the patrol couldn't keep up with us, so we two always rode far ahead. When we arrived alone at Spitzkopje, we discovered the nest was empty. The house was in excellent condition, but everything inside had been destroyed or looted. I found the remains of our murdered manager and quickly buried him on the farm. After two days, we rode back through Usakos to Karibib, and from there I returned back by train to Swakopmund.

As well as good commercial trade, 1905 and 1906 brought for Swakopmund and Lüderitzbucht numerous freehold property sales, which all had to be recorded by a notary in Swakopmund, and caused a lot of work. Our own construction department had been established by the Company under an architect and master builder sent from Germany. It employed many white artisans and natives, and built the first massive buildings from cement bricks and concrete; and the place soon began to look like a city.

New companies came to the country, shops and bars sprung out of the ground like mushrooms, and cabarets and music-hall came to Swakopmund. Money was earned and spent; and drinking sessions lasted through the night. In short: the place came to life.

In August and September 1906 I had to undertake an eight-week *Schutztruppe* Reserve Officer exercise, based at the Fourth Field Company in Otavifontein. The Herero war was more or less over, with the Hereros beaten and scattered in the great battle of Waterberg.

At the time, the companies in my exercise were commanded by military headquarters to return to their bases, and officers ordered to undertake constant patrols to disarm the stragglers still occupying Herero lands, and disperse them. The last two years in Swakopmund had brought a lot of hard work, often until late at night, so I saw these military exercises as a relaxing holiday. When the C.O., *Hauptmann* Hinsch, and his officers (who had only been in the country for a year) found out that I was an 'old Africa hand', a veteran of the Herero campaign and local expert, I received a warm reception and spent many pleasant hours in their circle.

After only two days I was sent with six riders and a six-horse mule-cart for a ten-day patrol. Soon afterwards I undertook a similar patrol.

After returning from this second patrol and a few days in service at Otavifontein, I was given a special task for a longer patrol. I was to travel on a prescribed route to Etosha Pan, along and then across the pan, and back to Otavifontein, to determine whether the water conditions would allow a better way to transport troops to Ovamboland. *Hauptmann* Hinsch, declared shortly before the departure of the patrol that he wanted to join the group 'as a guest', and that his presence would be off-duty and not connected to his official position.

In some ways I welcomed this, because Hinsch, was a passionate hunter, and I was hoping for some decent hunting opportunities at Etosha, and now because I had the C.O. accompanying me, no one would dare say of me 'he is going more for the hunting than for an official patrol.'

We rode over Grootfontein, Tsumeb, Lake Otjikoto, Sandhub, Narusib to Namutoni, to the beautiful forts erected on the eastern edge of Etosha Pan, with a protection detachment under the command of *Leutnant* Kaufmann.[45] After a convivial night spent there, one day's march brought us to the pan by way of Arikos and Rietfontein to Gunuhab. Everywhere at Etosha we found immense herds of game, springbok, gemsbok, hartebeest, and large herds of wildebeest (a type of small buffalo); and killed a lot. We lived only off wild game meat; and ended up bringing back to Otavifontein all the canned meat we carried along as supplies. What we didn't consume we immediately processed into biltong, and only the bones remained for the jackals.

---

[45] Probably Hans Kaufmann (1878-1914) who later served as a deputy district commissioner in the Caprivi Strip. Kaufmann was killed in the first weeks of the First World War during the Battle of Tannenberg in East Prussia.

From Gunuhab we turned to the south, riding cross country, from one reputed watering place to the next. However, we found most to be dry, or to contain only enough water for our patrol, but nowhere near sufficient for a larger numbers of troops.

After leaving the last inadequate waterhole we were now already two days without water; the heat was tremendous, and our animals and some riders began to get tired. However, one day at noon while riding ahead with my natives, I saw Bushman women and children some distance away, and knew that we had to be near water. The wild Bushman is the most cunning and repulsive of all the natives; he lives only from hunting with bow and arrow, has no home and no possessions. Bushmen never live next to a watering hole, in order not to identify them to others and so as not to scare away wild animals—their source of food. When Bushmen in uninhabited areas give you directions to water, you follow them at your own risk, they are mostly false. These women also naturally tried to direct me in exactly the opposite direction; but after I had carefully explained to them, with no possibility of misunderstanding, that they and their children would lead me, running ahead of the horses, and that if they should try to lead me astray, I would hang them all from the next tree, they took me within half an hour to Ubib. This was a delightful waterhole in the shade of tall, wild fig trees, and contained a lot of water.

At the water hole sat about 50 Bushmen armed with bows and arrows. I rode up at a gallop in between them, and told them that we had not come with hostile intent and had done nothing to them. Then I invited them 'politely' (with a Browning pistol in my hand) to lay down their arms together under a tree, and asked them to help us water our animals from the waterhole, which was about five metres deep. The rest of the patrol arrived, and in this beautiful shady spot we quickly forgot the misery and tension of the last two days. After man and beast had drunk their fill, we rewarded the Bushmen for our hunting with rice, tea, sugar and tobacco, and they left, apparently very satisfied. We decided to spend the night here, the horses were in pasture quite close to the camp, and also needed a rest. That night I set a sentry on the camp and another with the horses. In order to give the men as much rest as possible, I had arranged just a single sentry with the horses; after his two hours the man on guard had about 150 metres to walk back to the camp and hand over to his replacement; and as the horses were tired, well-fed and next to water I knew they would not think of running away.

At 4am I was awakened by the sentry with the good news that all our horses had disappeared. I immediately realized that the animals did not run away, but had been driven off during the unguarded ten minutes of the guard changeover by the Bushmen, who had kept us under observation.

It was too dangerous my men to search for the horses on foot in the dense bush. No, I would force Mr Bushman to bring them back himself, and they would certainly appear soon to fetch water, because there was no other water-hole within about 50 kilometres.

Soon men appeared in groups of ten to twelve, carrying bows and arrows, and bearing large vessels (calabashes) to fetch water. To each party (in total about forty men had appeared) I explained that my horses had 'run away' about two hours ago, and there would not be a drop of water available to anyone until they went away, found the horses and quickly brought them back. I confiscated bows and arrows and calabashes, and amid a great deal of grumbling and whining that their wives and children would die of thirst, they withdrew. My assumption was true, and the sanctions worked: at ten o'clock that morning all the horses were back where the last sentry had left them, however not a Bushman could be seen. We could not ride out immediately because of the intense heat; we did so in the afternoon only with the greatest caution, as we expected to be shot full of arrows in the dense bush by the outwitted and angry Bushmen.

We taught them even more of a lesson by burning their weapons and calabashes.

After three days' march via Dabib we rejoined the Field Company in Otavifontein after a twenty-day patrol. After only a few days back, my eight-week exercise was over, and I returned refreshed and revived to my work in Swakopmund.

In Swakopmund in the meantime a pretty young typist, Emmy Zehle, had arrived from Hamburg to work at Carl Bödicker & Co.[46] Soon after my return I met her on the Company tennis courts, and in a short while she had captured my hard old bachelor's heart.[47] We were together a lot, playing tennis, on walks, riding, picnics, with invitations and dances, and by the time of her return to Hamburg in 1907, we were secretly engaged.

From Lüderitzbucht Mr. Ludwig Scholz was whisked to Berlin to manage the Company from there, and he was replaced in Lüderitzbucht as managing director by Mr Robert Stolz, my predecessor in the *DKG*.

I was appointed from Berlin as a delegate of the Supervisory Board of the Company. I was subordinate to Lüderitzbucht with its newly established branches at Aus and Keetmanshoop, and as a result for at least two to three weeks every three months I had to travel there for audits and meetings.

The Company had undertaken seal hunting at Cape Cross, including the demolition of the remaining guano camp after the English had cancelled Ehlers' contract. But in the south, there were seals that not only lived on the small islands belonging to the Union of South Africa, but could also be caught with steel nets. As this fishing was rewarding, Scholz, Stolz and I privately founded a limited-liability seal-hunting society. We bought for 20,000 marks in Hamburg a beautiful, seaworthy sailing cutter. It was well-equipped with its own power for machinery, and in the first two years' fishing seasons we achieved dividends of 80% and 100%.

While staying in Lüderitzbucht I learned a great secret: that the local District Officer, who was a great trouble-maker and an enemy of all commercial companies, intended to prohibit for at least two years all seal fishing at the coast. As no one else knew this intelligence, we hastily sold our boat—at full asking price—to a competitor who had long envied us. With the success of our two years in business we could really

---

[46] A German import-export company based in Hamburg.

[47] Mansfeld was thirty-five years old.

be quite satisfied. The same District Officer also instigated an evil, ugly court case against the *DKG* and caused one of the oldest settlers in the south, Radford,[48] to contest the Company's ownership of Lüderitzbucht (Angra Pequena) and the so-called Radfordbucht. Since Radford himself was too old and inexperienced, a straw man, Robert Blank[49] was put forward. A very wealthy man, Blank believed that he had already won the case, but neither he nor a great number of other people involved with its future profits was able to make the required payment of costs in advance. This nonsensical court case lasted more than two years. It caused us enormous trouble and hard work, and ended up naturally enough with a clear victory for the Company, a huge award of costs against the opponent and a fairly hefty snub for the District Officer.

By February 1908 I was well overdue for home leave, which had fallen due during the Herero War and for two years afterwards. I went home on S.S. *Kronprinz* via East Africa. From Cape Town and especially from Durban the steamer was filled to the last berth; I had a first class single cabin on deck and it was a wonderful trip, with pleasant travelling companions. We called at all the ports on the east coast, and with plenty of money in my pocket and a healthy bank account I let nothing escape me. I stayed in Naples for three days, in Rome for three days and then met my Emmy Zehle in Lucerne. She was visiting her sister Elly in Zurich, but had come to meet up with me in Lucerne. After three days there, we then travelled to her sister in Zurich, and from there after a few days, they went to Hamburg and I to my parents who now lived in Dresden.

As always for an expatriate, the months in Germany were a sequence of recovery, pleasures and joys, and gradually dwindled until they quickly vanished altogether. On July 31 1908 we were married. We took an eight-day honeymoon in Lübeck, Kiel and Copenhagen and sailed as a young couple to South-West Africa on 9 August 1908.

---

[48] David Radford, a sailor who settled in Namibia in 1862.
[49] Robert Blank (1869-?). Farmer and member of the Legislative Assembly.

After our arrival in Swakopmund we lived in a small house that my colleagues had rented for me at the former Jauch brewery, we had bought and transported with us all the furniture that we needed. I purchased from the Company a plot on the corner of Post[50] and Otavi Streets and as there were no architects in Swakopmund Emmy and I drew up plans for a private residential home, which we called *Villa Emmy*, which was built by a local master builder and contractor. We moved into our new home in 1909.

There was a lot of work waiting for me in Swakopmund, because in June 1908 a Cape boy who was working on the construction of the Lüderitzbucht to Keetmanshoop railway found diamonds at Kolmanskop near Lüderitzbucht, and an incredible diamond fever had set in.[51] Thousands of mineral licences were requested from our Company, which possessed the land and mining rights. They had to be issued, and often transferred again and again, and if a mistake was made the miners would be only to happy to blame us for allegedly massive losses.

As my colleague Schettler often had to spend weeks in the diamond areas, I stayed behind and managed this work alone; goods contracts, banking and land deals increased constantly, and the work often felt daunting. When Schettler returned, I had to go to Lüderitzbucht because business was booming for the branch there: new shops being built on the diamond fields, and a large new building constructed for a commercial and residential building society.

When I came to Lüderitzbucht at the end of 1908, Mr Stauch,[52] who was one of the first diamond miners, still lived in his tent in Kolmanskop. I went with him to search on the dunes for diamonds and

---

[50] Now Daniel Tjongarero Street

[51] The discoverer was a Coloured labourer named Zacharias Lewala, who was shovelling sand when he spotted a crystal; he had worked in Kimberley and immediately recognised it as a diamond.

[52] August Stauch (1878-1947). Stauch was a railway worker, the supervisor of Zacharias Lewala. Stauch became a millionaire, but was forced into bankruptcy following the collapse of his investments after the First World War.

within a quarter of an hour picked up ten beautiful stones lying in the gravel.

Countless diamond companies were founded, and shares traded on the Bourse (in the reception hall of a hotel) every day. We went in the morning for a drink in the hotel, bought one or two shares of any company for, say, five hundred marks per share. If they were up to 750 marks the following day, you sold them and trousered the profit of five hundred marks. It was incredibly busy, with some people making a fortune, and many others losing one again. At night, the miners sat in the bars, drinking only champagne, and playing cards with payment in rough diamonds.

This unsavoury life went on so long that the government founded the Diamond Board[53] and brought to an end any trading in rough diamonds. In March 1909 I took my wife to Lüderitzbucht, so that even she got a flavour of diamond fever. In June 1909, we travelled together to Tsumeb, where I had to sort out our local branch of the Company, and even went to Grootfontein, travelling there by a six-span mule cart. In Tsumeb I caught malaria again, but after a few months off I was well again thanks to a strong horse-quinine cure.

By the end of 1909 the first German South West provincial government had been created by the government. Half of the members were elected by the population and half appointed by the governor. I was appointed by the Governor as representative of the Company. At the same time local councils were also created for the bigger towns, Windhoek, Swakopmund, Karibib, Lüderitzbucht and Keetmanshoop, who had to manage local affairs with a mayor.

The National Council met usually twice a year, three to six weeks at a time, for which I had to stay in Windhoek. I often had a hard time at the meetings and some hard battles to fight; The Company possessed the mining rights in the diamond areas, and all third parties working the diamond fields needed to pay their respective taxes to them because of that. There was envy and hatred expressed against the

---

[53] The *Diamanten-Regie-Gesellschaft Des Südwestafrikanischen Schutzgebiets*, founded in Berlin in 1909, which created a monopoly for diamond sales.

Company, and others sought to challenge their rights and tried to persuade the government to arrange for special measures.

With the founding of municipalities a property-tax law also came into force that threatened to strangle the Company, with its immense holdings of land in Swakopmund and Lüderitzbucht. It was left up to the two communities to establish their town boundaries in order to form a development plan. So as to sting the Company for as much tax as possible, the towns had declared within their boundaries an area of land so absurdly large that even without the First World War it would have taken fifty years to build upon it, and the only solution was for the Company to cede a large part of the land to the ownership of the municipalities. The negotiations over, it took more than two years to complete the contracts and surveys, bringing more of the same daunting but exhilarating work. The biggest farm sale, which Schettler and I managed in 1909, was to the Liebig Company in Khomas Highlands, a tract of 400,000 hectares.

In 1909 I received from the Chairman of the Supervisory Board in Berlin, *Direktor* Koch of Deutsche Bank, a letter telling me that the Board had decided to appoint me as co-director of the Company in Berlin. However, he asked me to reply and say openly and honestly whether this was currently feasible, or whether the wider interests of the Company required that I remain at my post in the diamond fields. This was a difficult decision for me because the position of director in Berlin was very tempting, but I had to answer truthfully that my current role was more important for the longer-term interests of the Company in South-West Africa. I was then appointed as deputy director in the diamond fields.

At the end of 1909 the Berlin Board sent out an assessor, Dr Ratjen, to rule in the legal matters in all the contracts with the government, the municipalities and diamond companies. I worked with him for a long time in Lüderitzbucht to achieve the land transfers to the local municipality. My colleague Schettler had an interest in a diamond company whose rights had been challenged by the Company. In 1910 he was suspended from his position and resigned from the Company, and in his place came Dr. Reuning,[54] who had founded the *Deutschen Diamanten Gesellschaft* in 1909. He joined me as deputy director, and I worked well and harmoniously with him until 1921. But I did at the same time obtain a special sole power of attorney for cases when the two of us could not agree. Dr. Reuning, as a geologist, had the whole of mining and our own small tin, scheelite etc mine operations under him.

---

[54] Ernst Reuning (1881-1961). Later an associate professor at the University of Giessen, moving to South Africa in 1935. He was interned during the Second World War, and retired to Stellenbosch.

1910 diary

1910 diary

In February 1910 I undertook a ten-day trip by horse and bullock cart with a former *Schutztruppe* captain called Steinhausen, who came out for a German sheep-breeding society.

21 February 1910
12.40pm from Swakopmund via Otavi station. 7.40pm evening in Onguati.

22 February 1910
7.30am from Onguati, 10am Omaruru. Met *Hauptmann* Steinhausen.

23 February 1910
Afternoon, 3pm ox cart in direction Okombahe, evening thunderstorms and heavy rain.

24 February 1910
Rode out at 7am, rain. Cart 9.50am at Otjompaue North (Kemnitz Farm). River open water, good grazing. 4pm, cart set off, we arrived 5.10pm riding. 6pm in Johannesbank, plenty of water, 3 kilometre ride, cart arrived 8 am, outstpanned for night.

25 February 1910
5am cart, we rode out 5.45am. 7am Okarundu (Sager Farm) 7.15am (Sander) 7.30 last pondokkies of Okarundu (Bastards). Cart came 8.30am. Poor pasture, water far away on the other side of the river, deep waterhole. 3.15pm, cart further on, rode at 4.20pm. 5.20pm Kawab (*Graf* von Bentheim's Farm) beautiful landscape, Area with high forest cover, good pasture. Unsaddled about 3 kilometres behind Kawab, cart arrived 7pm, stop for night, rain overnight.

26 February 1910

All off at 6am, we arrived 7am at Okombahe, cart 8am. Outspanned at the end of the village, poor pasture at Okombahe, no open water in river. Practically the only thing the kaffirs grow in their gardens is tobacco. Set off again 4pm, very hard road, crossed the river five times, twice within a couple of kilometres. In Dawetsaub no pasture and no open water, abandoned settlements, outspanned in grass about three kilometres further on at 7.45pm. Heavy rain overnight. In the afternoon killed three puff-adders and five scorpions.

27 February 1910

Started at 7am, very difficult road, often going up steeply; beautiful landscape, high tree cover but grazing bad. 9am outspanned about six kilometres from Tsumtsaub, strong west wind, rain and thunderstorms. At 11.40 continued in the rain to Aubinhonis, where we arrived 12.40. Location very dry, poor pasture in an area away from the river. There is always open water here in the river, now just a six-metre-deep water-hole at the edge of the bank. A lot of kaffirs here with their cattle, but not growing anything. Heavy rain during the afternoon and night.

28 February 1910

We spent the morning at Aubinhonis because, according to the natives, there was neither pasture nor water further along the river, Lewater quite dry, and Hasselund spoiled by cattle. For the sake of the oxen we could not therefore carry on via Achas and Lewater but had to strike out across country and try to meet the track between Okombahe and Spitzkopje.

We started at 3pm, back up overlooking a wide sandy river for four kilometres, a very difficult path for waggons but good pasture. Then over a long limestone ridge, no grass, hard stony ground; over two small pans until we saw a wide river, beautiful grass, set camp at 7pm for the night.

1 March 1910

Away at 5.15, cross country to the waterhole at Arisis, could only drink, no pasture until we outstpanned at 9am at Amisse Pan. Pan empty, but by digging we got so much water that we could water the horses and fill our water barrels. Set off again at 3.40, and joined the Okombahe-Spitzkopje road at 4.50 about 5 kilometres west of large black domes, which run along the western edge of Tubussis. From there we followed the road to Spitzkopje until 6:50 in the evening when we outspanned for the night in good pasture.

2 March 1910

Began early at 4.30am, reached Kettelrivier at 5.10am; outspanned on the road and took the horses and oxen on a further 35 minutes beyond the river and over three hilly ridges to Gamgamka Pan to drink. Back at 6.50am.

Beautiful pasture all the way along, past Buruuburub Pan, two small vleis; at 9am outspanned at Kummikenbank Pan, lots of good water. There are many natives with large and small animals. After 2.30pm, we rode on for about 12 kilometres where we found the last small river and decent pasture, but from then on largely hard, dry ground. We rode up to the gates of Gross-Spitzkopje, but could not find a single blade of grass. We therefore retraced our steps and took the track leading east around Spitzkopje, riding until nine-thirty at night without finding grass. After the wagon had halted, we outspanned and immediately tied the oxen for the night. Strong wind during the night.

3 March 1910

At 5.15am we rode ahead for Spitzkopje, with the waggon going directly on the road to Sandamap. Spitzkopje dismal, not a blade of fresh grass; dam three-quarters full. Buildings dilapidated, roof coverings gone, all stolen. Even by the big river trees have dried up and withered away, apparently it has not rained here for three years. We rode to the waggon and caught up with them 10am at Job Job by the river between the two black koppies, where there are boreholes and good grass. We outspanned there for an hour and a half and let the animals graze, then went on five kilometres to Sandamap, beautiful fresh grass and the pans full of water. No game in the entire area, the following morning we found fresh lion tracks near the camp.

4 March 1910

We stayed in Sandamap during the morning and then at about 3.15pm went on further towards Guabib, about 16 kilometres to the fork on the track to Okombahe, we followed it for about 4 kilometres but at 8.15pm outspanned for the night by a river.

5 March 1910

Up at 5.20am, at 6am at the waterhole at Guimenas. At Kudubis at 8.20am, and the cart followed us there at 9.20am. At Kudubis while surveyor Jacobs measured up the Schmidt farms. Very beautiful countryside, two dams full of water.

6 March 1910

Cart remains at Kudubis, Steinhausen and I ride at 6am to Tumib, Springbokfontein, to the last dam bordering Tubussis. Countryside everywhere very beautiful, plenty of water in the two big dams at Tumib, some small dams by the road, no water at the big dam at Springbokfontein, but about a kilometre north-east lies the dam at Daunabis which again has plenty of water. On our way back two hours in the saddle to Tumib and back in the laager at Kudubis at 2.30pm.

7 March 1910

Cart at 5.30am, we set out 6.30am, watered 8.10am at Guimenas and on to a large dam about 7 kilometres before Guabib (the farm of G. Struys). Tolerably good pasture; outspanned by noon. Great heat, an incredible number of bushticks and biting flies that drove us away again around 3pm this afternoon. We went by Guabib at 6pm and outspan for the night about 5 kilometres further out.

8 March 1910

Rode out 6am, we arrive at Usakos 8am, cart follows, 10am.

Final destination of our trip.

9 March 1910
7am train back to Swakopmund.

Distances:

Omaruru – Okombahe	72 kilometres
Okobahe – Aubinhonis	32 kilometres
Aubinhonis – cross-country to the	
Okombahe-Spitzkopje road	35 kilometres
Okombahe-Spitzkopje road to Spitzkopje	45 kilometres
Spitzkopje – Sendamap	16 kilometres
Sandamap – fork on road	16 kilometres
Fork on road – Kudubis	15 kilometres
Kudubis – Springbokfontein and back 50 kilometres	
Kudubis – Guabib	24 kilometres
Guabib – Usakos	12 kilometres
Total	318 kilometres

Working for the Company

Working for the Company

In July 1910, the Company celebrated its twenty-fifth anniversary, and at our suggestion we observed the day in an appropriate manner in Berlin as well as in Swakopmund. We held in *Hotel Kaiserhof* a huge banquet for the heads of departments, heads of companies and also the craftsmen of Swakopmund, inviting altogether more than one hundred people, and for a long time afterwards everyone was talking about this celebration, the sort of feast that Swakopmund had never seen before.

As I have already mentioned, the Company had interests in guano and seal hunting in Cape Cross, and kept a white man there (a Swede) and the necessary natives. Water was not available in Cape Cross, and the Englishman's condenser was no longer usable; so in order to convey the necessary provisions and fresh water in casks, we chartered one of the Wörmann steamers travelling to Swakopmund, which then took a return load of guano and seal-skins each time. I always travelled on these steamers as 'supercargo', usually twice a year.

On 9 April 1911 our first son Werner was born in Swakopmund, and all Swakopmund celebrated the joyful event with us.

Swakopmund had now grown into a nice town; our house, which to start with had been on its own—at least 150 metres away from the nearest buildings to the east—was soon surrounded by other buildings. The big beautiful church and the school building emerged in the immediate vicinity, and opposite us Dr. Brenner,[55] who was a close and sincere friend, built his family home.

At home in the stable we kept a pair of beautiful horses which we rode for an hour every morning and on longer trips on Sundays; and a light two-wheeled carriage we had bought. Great conviviality prevailed between the traders and officials and their families, with many entertainments and dances, and there were often periods where not a

---

[55] Fritz Brenner, German pathologist (1877-1969)

day in the week passed without dinner guests in the house. Emmy went on about how she managed it with only native staff to help!

1911 brought many more unpleasant negotiations and even court cases with the government because of the diamond area and tax matters, and as a consequence Dr. Reuning and I often had to travel to Windhoek and Lüderitzbucht. The managing director of the Lüderitzbucht Company, Stolz, was sacked from his post for unauthorized diamond dealing; and since after a short time his successor was proven to be unreliable, by early 1913 there was yet another change in this position—each time requiring me to stay longer in Lüderitzbucht.

By the beginning of 1912 the time had come for a furlough for me again. We left the house in the care of reliable employees of the company, and travelled in March, this time in third class with one-year-old Werner, via the west coast.

Of course we thoroughly exploited this holiday at home, enjoying city life and taking advantage of everything that we were deprived of overseas: in Hamburg with my in-laws; in Dresden with my parents; and a lot of travelling in between. I had repeatedly to make reports for the Directorate in Berlin, and before you knew it, the time was up and we had to prepare to return to Africa. At the end of August 1912 we travelled back from Hamburg. We took with us a girl as a housekeeper, who stayed with us right up until the outbreak of war, but then broke her contract, leaving us in the lurch in an unpleasant way right at the time when Emmy (who was then expecting our second child) most needed her help.

As soon as I arrived in Swakopmund, Dr. Reuning took his home leave, so of course my work doubled again. I was travelling a lot to Windhoek and Lüderitzbucht to council meetings and supervising our branches in Tsumeb, Guhab and Okombahe.

During the holiday in Germany, I had a wisdom tooth removed through surgery, which had grown transversely. Shortly after arriving in Swakopmund I developed a painful tumour on the lower jaw, which was removed in hospital in Windhoek through surgery under anaesthetic. As the wound did not heal, it had to be repeatedly opened and scraped until finally at another, bigger operation in Windhoek, the doctor chiselled away at my jawbone from the outside and pulled from beneath the jaw the root of the tooth which the two idiots of surgeons had left in following the first operation in Dresden. Dr. Brenner then treated the wound, but for weeks afterwards it would not heal, and I was tormented terribly for almost two years.

The Company was building a massive, two-storey administration building, fully equipped with all mod cons, and at the same time a bigger building in Windhoek as a branch of the Company. We made proposals and drew up plans, which were then developed in Berlin by an architect, and the board in Berlin approved them. By 1914 the project had reached a stage when construction would begin later that year. And then war broke out. Dr. Reuning returned mid-1913 from Germany and return, became engaged while overseas and married a few weeks later in Swakopmund, and at the end of the year the manager of the Banking Department, Kamieth, also came back married from his home leave.

One of my best employees, the manager of the goods department, Gogarten, went on leave at the beginning of 1914, could not come back due to the outbreak of war, and fell on the field of honour for his Fatherland.

German South-West Africa in the war

German South-West Africa in the war

At the outbreak of World War I in 1914, I found myself as a director of the *Deutsche Kolonial Gesellschaft für Süd West Afrika* in Swakopmund.

Previously, Reserve and Territorial forces in the colony, conscription, leave applications and extensions were all under the control of the responsible unit in Germany. In order to ease and simplify the previous cumbersome system, in 1913 the authorities at home assigned this control to the *Schutztruppen-Kommando* in Windhoek.

The Reserve and Territorial officers from military units based in Germany were encouraged to resign and transfer to the *Schutztruppe* Reserve. I followed that process, and was as a result at the time of the outbreak of war a *Leutnant* in the *Kaiserlichen Schutztruppe für Südwest Afrika*. Only in 1919, when regulated postal traffic was again possible with Germany, did I learn that I had been promoted to *Oberleutnant* in July 1914, and to *Hauptmann* in April 1915.

We received the war declarations of Britain and France against Germany on 5 August 1914, and at the same time a cable from the foreign ministry to the government: 'The colonies are not included in the state of war.' Since the attitude of the Union of South Africa was doubtful anyway, the government and troop headquarters ordered a general mobilization.

All too soon this measure turned out to be correct, because General Louis Botha[56] felt committed in the interest of England to go to war with the neighbouring German colonies. Since Botha's intention brought him into direct conflict with a large proportion of the Boer population, he did not hesitate to submit a forged map to Parliament. In it, Botha showed the German military post of Nakop, which was permanently manned and lay on the northern bank of the Orange River;

---

[56] Louis Botha had been a Boer leader during the Anglo-Boer War, and became Prime Minister of South Africa in 1911.

however, Botha marked it as being situated on the southern side of the Orange River, and thereby gave the impression that the Germans had already invaded Union territory. The Orange River was the border. A rebellion by Botha's opponents was soon ruthlessly suppressed by force of arms; Botha had achieved his purpose and was master of the situation.

On 6 August, I received my draft notice, to report immediately to the Sixth Field Company in Okanjande. All Reserve and *Landwehr* troops were simultaneously called up, and began moving out to their destinations within the country the next morning. By the evening of the same day a government order came out calling up members of the militia, so that only women, children, and a couple of old men unfit for service were left in Swakopmund. In contrast, at the time in Swakopmund there were five hundred natives and in particular two hundred Cape boys engaged in bridge construction, who immediately declared themselves as Union citizens. The Mayor of Swakopmund was in Windhoek and the nervous district magistrate did not consider it within his power to take action against this ill-considered action of the government. Therefore we did, my colleague Dr. Reuning, deputy mayor Günther, and I: bypassing the district magistrate to telegraph at night to the Governor that, for the protection of women and children and property, at least the Reserve troops should be allowed back to Swakopmund. At 2am, then, the orders concerning the militia were cancelled by telegraph.

On 8 August at 7am we departed by train from Swakopmund. My wife and my little 3½ year-old son Werner remained in Swakopmund.

I made it to Utjiwarongo on the evening of 9 August, and joined the company on the morning of 10 August at Okanjande. The company was on manoeuvres at the time war was declared, and had remained in Windhoek, so just the company commander, *Hauptmann* Petter, and another two officers were available to evacuate all the stores and ammunition.

I was to remain as commander at Okanjande. Naturally I was very displeased, and I hoped to find an opportunity soon to leave such a boring post and join the troops at the front line. The very next day a telegram came from the headquarters in Windhoek ordering me to report immediately to the transport division in Karibib. When I arrived there it appeared that this was wrong, and that I was posted to the 2nd Reserve Company under *Hauptmann* Erich Müller ('Jumbo' Müller), where I started my service as a leader of the first cavalry column on the morning of 13 August.

The following events are set out partly just in the form of diary entries. On 15 August, *Major* Ritter arrived to visit the company and brought as new company commander *Hauptmann* (retired)—and farmer—von Bennigsen, so Müller (a gunner) had to take over the 2nd Field Battery. At the same time my company received orders to occupy Okawayo as a new base the following day.

16 August 1914

Pastor Heyse held a very tedious morning field service in Karibib for the company. In his sermon he held up the Boers to our men as an example of good soldiers, because each Boer advanced into the field with the Bible in his pocket. He aroused the general displeasure of the company, and we officers were even then making plans to avoid any further sermons by the good pastor. He was later captured during the skirmish at Pforte and sat out the rest of the conflict. At three the next morning the company left for Okawayo under my command as senior officer. (*Hauptmann* von Bennigsen had over-enthusiastically celebrated his arrival and was somewhat indisposed, so he followed us the next day in a carriage).

17-19 August 1914

Setting up the base at Okawayo, care of horses, riding, close-order drill by squad, shooting and parades.

20 August 1914

On 20 August, I was ordered to investigate the water and grazing resources on the farms Gross- and Klein-Aukas and Tsawisis, about sixty-four kilometres from the coast; that is, to determine whether the company could be moved there. In Usakos I spent several hours with Emmy and Werner, who had come along from Swakopmund, then rode to each farm in turn, returning to Okawayo at noon on 23 August.

24-25 August 1914
Major Ritter held a company inspection near Johann Albrecht Höhe and a combat exercise, testing the officers; my squad performed particularly well.

26-29 August 1914
Service in the company, riding, shooting, drill.

30 August 1914
Following my positive report on water and pasture in Aukas, an order came that the company should transfer its outpost there. All preparations have been made.

1 September 1914
As there were two wells to be repaired at Aukas (the place was uninhabited) I went there via Karibib and Usakos with an advance-party of twenty specially-chosen troops (engineers, well-drillers etc) and a waggon. In Usakos I could requisition the necessary hand tools, wire ropes, well buckets and drinking troughs for the horses, and by 3 September we had the wells in order. The company arrived in Aukas on the evening of the same day.

4-11 September 1914
Finished setting up the laager, building small huts from bushes because it was very cold, cross-country riding, training the horses, and various patrols in the area.

12 September 1914
Emmy and Werner came back from Swakopmund, visited the camp at Aukas. I got to spend two days' leave with them in Usakos.

14-17 September 1914

On 14 September Müller-Artois, the director of *Otavibahn*,[57] told me in a deafening telephone call that an English cruiser had appeared off Swakopmund, and had shelled the radio tower. Swakopmund was evacuated by the civilian population, so Emmy, expecting our second child, could not return to Swakopmund with Werner, and travelled from Usakos on to Karibib, taking only a small bag containing enough essential clothing for two to three days. I galloped back to Aukas with a message to alert the company, and the order from headquarters to be ready to march. *Hauptmann* von B. rode to Usakos for a meeting by telephone with headquarters, and came back on the morning of 15 September with orders that the company march immediately to near Dorstreviermund, to complete our departure at 10pm, watering the horses in Ubib at 1.30am and then riding on for a further eight kilometres before unsaddling our horses to graze on sweet grass.

At 10pm the company set off to Dorstrevier station, and at the same time *Major* Wehle[58] departed by train. The whole way to Ubib was over very poor terrain, so we had to ride very slowly, ambling our way, and since the road from Ubib was even worse, the company remained at Dorstrevier for the night. It was horribly cold, the ground was rocky, there was no fire or water. On 16 September at 7am, the company pressed on towards Dorstreviermund, while I rode for Kubas with Reserve *Vicefeldwebel* Dr Reuning and six men, to set up a telephone connection with headquarters. The wires were simply draped down over trees and bushes. There was no water anywhere, so at one point in order to ground the cable, we simply dug a hole and all eight men pissed in it, and the grounding worked then. We arrived in Dorstreviermund at seven o'clock in the evening. The company had set up camp under high trees (there were no tents during the entire war, we always camped out

---

[57] The Otavi Mining and Railway Company (*Otavi Minen- und Eisenbahn Gesellschaft*)

[58] Karl Wehle was a *Bezirksamtmann* serving in several districts in colonial Namibia.

in the bush under 'Mother Nature') there was a delightful echo, good water in the area and excellent pasture for the animals; but many awful, dry, sandy pans and—which was worse— millions of disgusting green caterpillars crawled everywhere under the blankets and uniforms, causing terrible itching and blisters all over our bodies.

18 September 1914

A message came on 18 September that Englishmen had landed in Walvis Bay (the message was incorrect, since they had landed in Lüderitzbucht) so a column of men under *Leutnant* Müller was ordered to Goanikontes.

21 September 1914

On September 21, I received orders to take three officers and eleven men and set up outposts in Salem, about thirty-five kilometres downriver.

22 September 1914

On 22 Sept, we rode off at 7am to Horebis and Dieptal, arriving at Salem at noon. Because the advantage of Salem was not clear, I rode with a small group through Riet, alongside 'Langen Heinrich' (an enormous mountain), over the Nabas River to Modderfontein, and finally back to the rest of my men at Salem, fifty-four kilometres all told. Riet seemed the most appropriate place for an outpost because Riet provided a view extending as far as Goanikontes from the river near 'Langen Heinrich'; and if the enemy approached from Swakopmund, he would have to come through Riet because of the availability of water.

23 September 1914

I received permission from the company to relocate the outpost to Riet, and moved there immediately with my fourteen men; we made camp at not far from the Swakop River, beneath tall trees about six hundred meters from the small farm settlement of the Bielenbergs.

That same afternoon I received orders to identify all potential water sources downriver from Goanikontes in order to quickly render them unusable if the enemy advanced. This was not much use in my view, because wherever there is a dry river bed there is water: you only need to dig down a few metres and you will find fresh running water.

I was at Riet from 24 September to 4 November 1914. It was ordinary company service, as well as constant patrols, building roads, and also identifying potential combat positions in case of attack. Our camp was under trees, and gradually we collected wooden slats and old corrugated iron from Jakelswater train station and an old railway shed in Riet, and built some protective cover against rain and the heat of the sun. We cooked communally in a single pot, and I got beer and schnapps from the Bielenbergs whenever I could, to share with my men. Except for one, they were all good fellows.

In order to be able to escape the enemy over 'Langen Heinrich' mountain if necessary, I tried to find a route across the mountain that was feasible for riders. Now this was an almost impossible task but, thanks to *Unteroffizier* Rucktäschel, after days of patrols we finally succeeded in finding a path which we then expanded (with difficulty) to create a passable road over the mountains to Tinkas. This reduced the time to get around the mountain by more than six hours. I dubbed a small conical hill, about three hundred metres high, *Wehleberg*, and selected it as an observation post. From there a sentry overlooked the whole river, the land in front of it and the selected combat positions, and could keep in communication through flag signals.

From a detachment of Basters under *Hauptmann* Hiller Gertrin-Gärtringen which was near Tinkas, I received six Basters and a Baster sergeant (men from Rehoboth)[59] who were mainly to be used as

---

[59] *Hauptmann* Baron Hiller von Gärtringen, was the German *Bezirksamtmann* (magistrate) of Rehoboth. All able-bodied Baster men were called up, in the face of fierce opposition from Baster leaders; this was mitigated somewhat by German assurances that Baster troops would only be used in non-combatant roles in the Rehoboth district, and the conscripts became increasingly displeased after they were moved outside the district.

despatch riders, and who undertook night sentry duty at the camp alternating with my own troops. Several times I rode seventeen kilometres to the remote railway station at Jakalswater to communicate with the Company headquarters by telephone; and from there I even managed to telephone my wife in Karibib.

Patrols from other units, and from the detachment based at the Goanikontes outpost passed around here, so I often had many officers as guests at my table—which consisted of an old trunk.

Once a situation occurred which, while hilarious for us, was most embarrassing for the fellow affected. *Hauptmann* von B., the company doctor, Dr. Mäntz, and *Leutnant* Werner came by on a patrol and stayed over night with me. I always gave the daily password to the camp guard at 6pm, and since no stranger had any business hanging round in the vicinity of the camp, there were clear instructions to shoot when an intruder would not respond to a challenge and request for the password.

Of course, I always gave my guests the daily password and also told them that our luxurious latrines were two hundred metres away, beyond the river. *Leutnant* Werner, an effeminate, spoiled little gentleman, a high-ranking government official, had some stomach trouble at night, possibly from my somewhat rough evening meal, and needed the lavatory. He knew the way to the sentry-box, but that night the Basters were on guard, who did not recognise him; they immediately ordered him to halt, and Werner saw a gun aimed at himself. He gave his name and rank. "Anybody could say that," came the reply. "What's the password?"

Oh dear.

Werner did not know the password; so the guard grabbed him, and dragged him to me just as Werner's digestion was rapidly approaching danger-point. I had already been woken by the shouting, and freed W. quickly, but I think it was already too late, as he sped away. The rest of us laughed immoderately and—being somewhat malicious—the next morning I heaped praise on the sentries.

Since we could not get any fresh meat from company HQ, on 13 October I rode with a few men and a waggon to Tinkas to try to shoot a gemsbok. We didn't see any game at all until I shot a nice fat male zebra in Tinkas Gorge one evening. Our people called zebras 'trapp-trapp' because of the rattle of their hard hooves on the rocks. When we came back to the camp we prepared some lovely zebra steaks which all tasted good. Just one man, the only regular artilleryman at the outpost, said that he did not eat horsemeat. He had a large nose, and was the only one who had not brought a horse with him for recreation.[60]

"Relax, my boy," I said, "all the more for us. Feel free to fill up on corned beef and rice." Later the same day I noticed that the stables were in a dreadful mess and bawled out the men. When I passed by the stores, which lay about 30 metres from my hut, I heard this zebra-despiser say to the other troops, "There you go, first he eats trapp-trapp, and then he shouts at us." Somehow the chief magistrate of Karibib, an uncompromising lawyer; a reserve officer (but one who was very happy living in his beautiful home, with comfortable beds and good food) heard of my iniquity. It was forbidden to shoot zebras; I was ordered to headquarters, where the commissariat gave me a letter warning me not to repeat the offence.

The pettiness infuriated me, and I answered that I acknowledged my guilt where this abhorrent crime was concerned. I added that I would like to swap my position with the chief magistrate of Karibib, and then to see if after several weeks lying in the dust instead of a warm bed, and without any meat for him and his men, he would not also be tempted to shoot a zebra. That was roughly my reply; headquarters understood the message correctly, and I later heard that they sent just a brief acknowledgement to the chief magistrate.

On 24 October 1914 I received six days' leave to go to Karibib to attend to various *DKG* business matters, and to visit my wife and son. After several bombardments by a cruiser Swakopmund had been evacuated, and the railway line to Rössing torn up. This left large compounds belonging to various companies which they had not been able to empty because of the hasty destruction of the railway line, and in

---

[60] The inference is that the artilleryman was Jewish; in Nazi Germany Jews were forbidden to go horseback riding.

many places these fell into the hands of the enemy. Our company alone had lost about 400,000 marks' worth of goods in this way. The company office had been transferred to Karibib together with my secretary *Fraulein* Bügen, and the three employees who were not conscripted. Our important company documents were preserved almost entirely by two employees, especially Buchholz, who concealed them during the evacuation of the offices and over a number of evenings removed the files and transported them at night by mule cart to Rössing and from there by train to Windhoek.

From 25 October to 3 November I spent quiet days in Karibib with Emmy and Werner, once again enjoying a decent life sleeping in a bed. I learned about the punitive expedition our troops undertook to Naulila under *Major* Franke, and the storming of these forts in retaliation for the treacherous killing of three of our officers by the Portuguese.[61]

On 3 November 1914, I returned to Riet. *Leutnant* Müller, who relieved me, took over command of the outpost, and on 4 November I returned with my men to the main company in Dorstreviermund, arriving back on the morning of 5 November.

The stay at the company bored me: with the eternal monotony, riding, drill, parades, etc. I was bored and I hoped soon to get my own command again.

On November 12, we received the news that our commander, *Oberstleutnant* von Heydebrek, had been killed during a test firing of rifle grenades, after one exploded prematurely. This was a great loss for the troops, because von Heydebrek was an excellent leader, while some of those who succeeded him in the years following would perhaps not be. His successor was *Major* Franke (promoted to *Oberstleutnant*). Franke had been the most intrepid officer in the Herero campaign (*Pour*

---

[61] On 19 October 1914, German troops crossed into Angola without authorisation from the Portuguese. The Portuguese escorted the column to Fort Naulila, a border post, where a dispute between the Portuguese and Germans ended in the death of three German officers. On 31 October German soldiers carried out a punitive raid on the Portuguese outpost at Cuangar, killing eight.

le Merite[62]); a brilliant company commander and battalion commander, but was no strategist.

On 14 November, came news from Windhoek that *Leutnant* Werner had been transferred from the company to the garrison at Johann-Albrechtshöhe; a quiet, comfortable, undemanding position in well-appointed quarters, very much to Werner's taste. Werner had been posted to the outpost in Goanikontes before me, and I replaced him there in turn. On 15 November at four in the morning I marched off to Salem with two officers, 14 mounted troops and a military waggon, via Horebis and Dieptal. We stayed overnight in Salem and then continued the following day through Riet, Gawieb and Witport to Husab, and then on 17 November by Haigambghab to Goanikontes, where I arrived at 7am after a ride of 118 kilometers.

Goanikontes was the closest outpost to Walvis Bay. Located between Rössing and Swakopmund, *Hauptmann* Scultetus[63] was based with a small contingent to guard the coast. At the end of September Scultetus had gone at night to Walvis Bay, where he captured the police sergeants, and destroyed their steam launch. The only reason Scultetus could not capture the magistrate was that each night he retreated out to the cruiser, moored in safety off the shore. The Hottentots of Sandfontein (five kilometres west of Walvis Bay) were constantly attracted to the abandoned town of Swakopmund and looted the shops. Scultetus captured thirty of the wretches and had them hanged in Rössing. Now there were still in Walvis Bay four leading villains—whites—who made common cause with the Hottentots, and we wanted to get them.

On 19 November at 6pm I rode along with all the off-duty troops, *Leutnant* Hundsdörfer[64] and Dr Reuning to the eight-kilometre

---

[62] The 'Blue Max', a Prussian military award with which Franke was honoured for his services during the Herero War.

[63] Oscar Scultetus (1879-1950).

[64] This is probably C. L. Hans Hundsdörfer (1883-1959) whose gravestone at Swakopmund shows that he was a Reserve *Hauptmann* during the First World War.

mark, where we met *Hauptmann* Scultetus. At 5am the following morning we were joined by reinforcements from Rössing, and rode to Swakopmund, to Kayser's market gardens. Then after dark we rode along the shore, past the whaling station towards Walvis Bay in the direction of Sandfontein until the first big dune. There we met *Leutnants* von Milkau[65] and Könitz, from Ururas, with seven more men.

At dusk on 20 November, in thick fog, I galloped furiously towards the rambling old wooden houses (Bollmann & Kemp) situated on the lagoon in Walvis Bay. I surrounded the houses with six men from the south, Scultetus from the north and von Milkau from the east, and in the two houses we found the four we were looking for (one former American, one Portuguese, an African and a Cape boy). They surrendered at the end of a Browning and were captured. These men went back with our people towards Sandfontein.

While Scultetus, von Milkau and I were riding, we were joined by a missionary, who told us that the cruiser was lying in Walvis Bay, so we could not ride back along the shore. And meanwhile the fog lifted and the cruiser became visible, so we thought it was about time we left Walvis Bay. As we rode away, the cruiser fired a grenade towards the area, but it did not hit us.

After we ate some breakfast and watered the horses in Sandfontein, we set out on journey way back along the Pluem river. In Rooibank we parted, von Milkau took the prisoners first from Ururas because they had to walk on foot, and I rode straight to Goanikontes where we arrived dead tired at five in the morning after a 140 kilometre journey. The next day *Leutnant* Hundsdörfer marched back to headquarters with his troops.

On 23 November I rode with one trooper to Swakopmund. I left at 8am; at 11am I was at the eight-kilometre line, an English battle cruiser was anchored in front of Swakopmund, so I could not ride any further until 2am. Our house in Swakopmund was still intact. I brought two large suitcases packed with clothes and laundry down to the door, and then later that night the owner of the farm at Goanikontes picked

---

[65] *Freiherr Leutnant* Hans von Milkau died at Rehoboth 27 April 1916.

them up and transported them to Emmy in Windhoek. I did a similar thing in later rides, usually at night, and so saved at least some of our belongings.

Until 4 January I commanded the outpost in Goanikontes, and kept just brief daily notes of the little incidents in this period that happened besides the usual services, patrols etc.

24 November 1914

Leutnant von Milkau brought me six Baster soldiers as dispatch riders.

25 November 1914

A big visit: *Oberleutnant* Venuleth[66] and his wife; *Leutnant* Schmatz and his wife (the latter both turned out later to be traitors, he was reportedly later shot for it in Germany), Scultetus, Winkelmann and Brauer, all stayed overnight and in the evening we celebrated vigorously with a few drinks.

27 November 1914.

With Scultetus, Winkelmann and Brauer to Swakopmund for the troops to requisition everything possible. Pulled back to eight kilometres outside Swakopmund, and were back in Goanikontes on 28 November.

29 November 1914 to 5 December 1914

Constant guarding, watch and patrols.

7 December 1914

I was back in Swakopmund, and met the four prisoners from Walvis Bay at Goanikontes in the evening.

---

[66] This is probably Reserve *Oberleutnant* Carry Venuleth, who was tried after the war for condemning to death in a hastily-convened court an elderly Bushman couple whom one of his patrols had captured.

9 December 1914

Leutnant von Könitz brought seventy-two Hottentot prisoners from Ururas. I had to watch them for a couple of days, and then we took them through Rössing to Windhoek together with the four whites, and delivered them.

11 December 1914.

On the orders of *Hauptmann* Scultetus, I left at 7am with nine mounted troopers, with the aim of meeting him in Walvis Bay before riding south to survey the area for hostile natives. We broke at Rooikop to water the horses and allow them to rest, and arrived in Walvis Bay at 6pm. The place was deserted except for some Hottentot women, who told us that Scultetus had already gone back to Swakopmund. We stayed the night at the whaling station.

12 December 1914

We rode south along the coast to Wortel and Frederiksdam, leaving at 5am, but found neither water sources nor natives. In the evening we went back to the whaling station.

13 December 1914

There was no sign of the cruiser, so we moved along the shore to Swakopmund, arriving there at 10am. At noon the cruiser appeared off Swakopmund, so I sent my men to wait for me six kilomtres outside town, while one trooper and I remained to observe from the street corner by the *Hotel Bismarck*. The cruiser launched a boat with a white flag. The boat crew came ashore and set the wood store of Wörmann, Brock & Co. on fire. In fury, we fired after the retreating boat before heading at speed out of the cloud of smoke to the rendezvous, where the troops and I stayed overnight.

14 December 2014

Since the cruiser had disappeared from the coast at Swakopmund, we rode back early to Goanikontes. We spent the following few days with non-stop patrols to Ururas and towards Walvis

Bay, keeping watch and requisitioning and loading fresh vegetables, up to eighty cents per week, for the troops. We received our food in Goanikontes from the commissariat, and even though our location was surrounded by vegetable farms, who sent a constant supply of fresh food to the commissariat, we always received wizened potatoes and wilted vegetables. It was pointless to complain, and even my official memo about it was unsuccessful.

20 December 1914

Emmy and Werner arrived for a Christmas visit to Goanikontes, I fetched them from Rössing by waggon.

24 December 1914

Christmas celebration with Emmy and Werner, and I had a party for my men before that.

25 December 1914

Several more officers visiting, along with *Frau* Venuleth, and a Christmas meal in the evening all together.

26 December 1914

I went out for a ride with all the troopers who were not posted to duty, just to blow away the last traces of Christmas spirits. We had ridden about two kilometres, and were near Endklippe when suddenly a rider came galloping to us with the message that thirteen steamships were lying off Walvis Bay, and about four hundred men and many horses had already landed. Back galloping to Goanikontes to speak to headquarters by telephone; Emmy and Werner straightaway to Rössing by waggon and from there by train to Karibib. All women from the farms in the district were ordered to evacuate to Karibib, several farmers conscripted into the militia and, and we carried out patrols towards Walvis Bay and Ururas.

I got a message that in Walvis Bay they had already erected more than four hundred tents and at least 1,500 men had been landed. We were on full alert, with all positions fortified, as of course we expected an attack any moment and I and my fourteen men had to hold the post as long as possible. We waited in vain; there were five days with nothing happening, but the Tommies were in no hurry and were probably poorly informed about our strength.

1 January 1915

Generalstabshauptmann Weck and Scultetus came from Windhoek to Goanikontes with twenty-three men. At five that afternoon thirty-seven of us rode off towards Walvis Bay. There were three Baster soldiers riding with us as grooms, but they were troublesome. As I did not trust the rascals, we left them behind (at my suggestion). The Basters of Rehoboth had very recently declared solidarity with our enemies and rebelled against us. At ten o'clock at night, we grouped in front of the '*Schwarzen Klippen*', behind the dunes, and since the English had not yet occupied the area, we stayed there overnight, with sentries posted on all sides.

2 January 1915

After discovering that there were still no enemy troops visible, we rode in loose battle formation towards the highest dune, taking it at a sharp gallop. *Hauptmann* Wecke, Scultetus and I climbed the steep sandbank and were rewarded with a wonderful view over the hustle and bustle in Walvis Bay, which lay ahead of us, about three hundred metres away. There were many steamers and a battle-cruiser in the harbour, a host of tents, magazines, horses, seven tugs continuously landing troops—and sentries everywhere. By 7am we had seen everything we wanted, and rode back to Nonidas, where we watered the horses, and back to camp by midday.

3 January 1915

The English cruiser went to Swakopmund overnight; after it had left, we rode into Swakopmund; *Hauptmann* Weck wanted to visit in order to inspect the damage caused by the bombardment to the bridge, power station and waterworks. We also laid mines. We came back to Rössing, arriving at about 7pm; and then after long discussions over a communal meal I had a wonderful rest: sleeping like a lord in the saloon car of a director of the railway, who was there by chance.

4 January 1915

I rode with my men back to Goanikontes at 7am. A company to man the forward posts was formed under the command of *Hauptmann* Scultetus using men from the 2nd Reserve Company and the coastal defence unit, with *Hauptmann* von Bennigsen coming to the Karibib district. At three o'clock that afternoon I rode with Scultetus to look for a suitable position to base the company, climbing over every mountain until we found a suitable place on the banks of the Swakop.

5 January 1915

At 8am the entire company came to Goanikontes. Immediately after watering the horses, I led them to the new camp.

6 January 1915

I went out with the *Hauptmann*, looking for a way through the cliffs which could give us an escape route from the new position in case of attack, a path which we could then make bigger.

7-12 January 1915

Extension and furnishing of the camp, fixing it up, splitting the company into squads, setting sentries, carrying out patrols. Reports from Rooibank that Australians were patrolling there.

12 January 1915

Scultetus, von Milkau and I rode with a column to *Schwarzen Klippen,* arriving at 10pm. While checking on the sentries overnight, I found two fast asleep; I immediately arrested them and sent them for trial in Windhoek.

13 January 1915

Left before daybreak to the great dune, stayed there observing until 8am and then back across to Goanikontes with all speed.

14 January 1915

News came early that the British were proceeding along the beach from Walvis Bay. Large numbers of troops came to Swakopmund, and Woker[67] detonated three mines; we laid them at the mouth of the Swakop River, and he set them off from inside an old piano packing-case buried in the dunes. Apparently the Tommies are in a bad way now. At the time, the small number of guards at the lighthouse captured nine splendid officers' horses, complete with saddles, whose riders had probably separated themselves involuntarily. Woker (an officer of the Wörmann Line), who had been part of the coastal defence unit, detonated one mine after the other, very carefully and calmly. In the ensuing chaos he then climbed out of his packing-case, hid until nightfall in the bushes growing in the Swakop, and arrived at the eight kilometre point[68] at 2pm. He estimated the enemy's losses from the mines at about fifty men.

Immediately after receiving the report, Scultetus rode with the second and third columns beyond the eight-kilometre line, and stayed there the following day. I was in the camp in a condition of high alert with the rest of the company. There were reports of seven hundred to eight hundred men in Swakopmund, a main camp built between the church and school, sentry posts put around the place up to four kilometres radius, and large wire structures erected.

16-19 January 1915

The usual patrols and keeping watch.

20 January 1915

Scultetus, Venuleth and von Milkau and sixteen men went with me and my men to Felseneck. The three of them went on in the

---

[67] Theodor Woker (1889-?), later the managing director of Wörmann Lines and mayor of Swakopmund.

[68] This refers to kilometre distance points on the railway line.

afternoon with their sixteen men eastward to Nonidas, and I followed with my men at seven o'clock that evening.

21 January 1915

At two o'clock in the morning we went a further three kilometres on, to a farmhouse and small hen-house on the banks of the Swakop that belonged to Fisker, the customs officer. The English used it during the day as a sentry post, and we wanted to have a go at playing an English sentry. Scultetus and von Milkau occupied the sniper's house and the hen-house, and I went with my men to the other side of the Swakop behind a high dune, from where there was a good view. At six in the morning the English field guard, arrived on horseback: one officer and twenty men. They halted in the riverbed about one hundred metres below the house, and sent one man forward as advance guard. He rode up towards our position, looking around in every direction, and then dismounted and began climbing the narrow path from the river to the farmhouse.

The first shot from Scultetus was the signal to open fire, and the ensuing gunfire on the retreating guard from the occupants of the house brought down six men. At the first shot, I galloped across the riverbed, and when I arrived at the high wall in front of the house, the English scout tumbled helter-skelter down the path and collapsed to the ground in front of my horse. When I jumped down from my horse the soldier rose with his hands up. Surprised, I called out "Hallo! I thought you were killed!" whereupon he answered, horrified, "God damn it, you think I'm going to be killed for three shillings a day?"

We had captured four good horses and our first prisoner, whom I immediately sent back with two men to the agreed collection point, a few kilometers upriver. The rest of the guards had gone back to Swakopmund. Scultetus and I rode towards Swakopmund with my platoon laid out in an extended skirmish-line, until we were within range of the machine-guns mounted in the water-towers; then came the order 'turn back', and we rode away at a gentle trot.

Suddenly we saw two cavalry companies riding out of Swakopmund in close formation; Scultetus declared that it might be impertinent for our thirty men to attack two companies of cavalry (two hundred men). Next, he ordered "Towards the enemy, at the gallop!" This caused them to wheel around immediately, and they vanished into Swakopmund, leaving us laughing as we turned back again and rode to our rendezvous-point.

A squad from the company was waiting on guard for us at the eight-kilometre point. The camp there was on a raised hill, which offered a good view of Swakopmund, and was occupied every day by an officer and thirty men. Since the English withdrew all their sentries to Swakopmund when it got dark, our guard returned to the camp at the eight-kilometre point. In the camp I tried to interrogate the prisoner, who was very uncommunicative. However, by asking neutral questions I finally managed to get information out of him that there were over eight hundred tents in Walvis Bay, each of which was occupied by ten to fifteen men.

25 January 1915

The company depot was moved to Felseneck, about 8 kilometres from Goanikontes. On the 25th of January, at four o'clock, Scultetus and I rode with my men and von Milkau with the second column towards Swakopmund to see if and by how far the enemy had already advanced. We were back at Nonidas by 8pm, with the the rest of the company due to arrive back at eleven o'clock that evening.

26 January 1915

At 2am von Milkau and I rode with our columns to the five-kilometre point and occupied the cliffs there. Venuleth and Hundsdörfer occupied positions at kilometers seven and eight, it was a cold foggy night. At six in the morning an enemy patrol of five men under a sergeant came to my position from the Swakop. The sergeant rode forward, carefully gazing around in all directions, until he came too close to us and was shot off his horse. He was badly wounded and, as more enemy forces were coming upon us at the same time, I let him lie behind our cliffs out of the line of fire. von Milkau and I went forwards to some sandstone cliffs at the three-kilometre point with our men, but the enemy was approaching us from three sides and the cruiser lying at anchor was firing at us, so we had to go back to the eight-kilometre point with the other columns. The enemy tried to attack us here, but broke off the fight and went back to Swakopmund. That left our company with nothing to do, so they rode back to Felseneck, and I stayed behind at the eight-kilometre point to keep watch. We had to leave the wounded English sergeant, and since I assumed that his men would miss him and come to fetch him, I left him something to eat and a field-bottle of water, and put a handkerchief up as a white flag on the rocks. English patrols came up several times a day to the seven-kilometre point, but they did not come to collect their wounded. I therefore decided to take him back to the camp in the evening, and sent for a cart and a stretcher. However, our doctor, who came to examine the man, considered it impossible for him to survive the transport to Karibib; but only an immediate operation could save his life.

Scultetus, therefore, decided to send the doctor and an *Unteroffizer* under a white flag of truce to Swakopmund. I followed their progress from my position, keeping them in my view for their protection. English officers received the pair at the three-kilometre point: the sergeant had not been missed. The English sent a field ambulance immediately and thanked us for our gallantry; they promised to do the same for us if a similar case arose. We returned to Felseneck.

27 January 1915

The Emperor's birthday. At six o'clock in the morning, field service by the Roman Catholic priest Father Jacobs (whom we got thoroughly drunk at the celebration that night). In the afternoon, there was a company parade, a speech by Scultetus and three cheers for the Emperor.

30 January 1915

At four o'clock in the morning Scultetus, von Milkau and I rode with our squads to Nonidas.

31 January 1915

At four o'clock in the morning we rode to the beacon point at the six-kilometre point and took up positions to mount an ambush. By eight o'clock there was no sign of any enemy troops, so we rode back to the camp.

1 February 1915

At 2 o'clock in the morning my company was on guard again at the eight-kilometre point. Enemy scouts were repeatedly coming up to the seven-kilometre point. Before returning to the camp in the evening, I made it a rule to ride with two men along the railway as far as the three-kilometre point to find out enemy positions; and at the same time an *Unteroffizer* led a patrol along the higher ground on the opposite side, and rode back along the same route. Tonight the *Unteroffizer* made the mistake of crossing the railway line and riding back behind us. In the half-dark, we had to assume that we were being pursued by a hostile patrol. We galloped behind a small hill, and although my men were about to fire, I felt uncertain and stopped them in time, just before we shot over the hill at our own troops. The *Unteroffizer* got a pretty comprehensive chewing-out, and ended up looking like a complete idiot.

2 February 1915

Our camp was moved to the other side of the Swakop river.

3 February 1915

My squad's turn to stand guard at the 8 kilometre point.

6 February 1915

The squad went back to Nonidas in the evening, arriving at nine o' clock. Fed and watered, and rested until reveille at midnight.

7 February 1915

We set off at one in the morning. Venuleth's company went to the four-kilometre point on the Otavi railway line and laid mines there.

von Milkau's company was supposed to be in position beyond the limestone cliffs at the Swakop at the four-kilometre point, but they came up on Venuleth's company in the dark, and ended up being shot at. Scultetus, Hundsdörfer and I with our two companies rode across Larz's farm[69], crossing the Ururas road, and taking up positions on the highest dune in the dune belt by the Swakop.

At four-thirty in the morning, we heard firing from Venuleth's company; we could hardly believe it, as we could not imagine that the enemy was behind us. The dunes approximately two hundred metres ahead of us were occupied by the English, about two companies strong. At five o' clock in the morning we opened fire, and the English immediately responded with a volley of shots, and machine guns. The enemy reinforced and tried to bypass our left flank, so at six o' clock we had to fall back. At the foot of the dunes we had to gallop at high speed across completely open, unprotected country, under fierce machine-gun fire from two companies of enemy troops, until we reached a small hill on the Lartz farm on the north side of the Swakop. We came under fire there too, and as the enemy gained strength we were forced to abandon that position and go back to the eight-kilometre point. The enemy attacked us there too, but took some hits and finally pulled back to Swakopmund. At nine o'clock I went back to keep watch from the eight-kilometre point; there was a huge commotion in Swakopmund.

8 to 10 February 1915
Patrols, sentry duty and the usual camp duties.

11 February 1915
Watching again from the eight-kilometre point. In the evening on the way to the three-kilometre point I came under close fire; I was being nosey, and the enemy post was hidden. Close? Too close.

---

[69] A dairy farm just outside Nonidas.

13 February 1915

At half-past three in the morning I rode out again with Scultetus and my company towards Walvis Bay. We arrived at the *Schwarzen Klippen* at nine o'clock. The position was apparently occupied by the enemy, as we could see fires nearby through the fog. We retreated a kilometre away; it was difficult to orient ourselves in the darkness because of the dense fog and rain, so we waited for daybreak. Everything was in readiness, we had sentries posted on all sides, and the horses just had their saddle-girths slackened.

14 February 1915

At four o'clock in the morning we saw *Sergeant* Adomeit,[70] who had been patrolling alongside us until we lost him in the night. He reported that the cliffs were not occupied. Straight away we rode over to the dunes, and observed from there until half-past eight, when we began riding back. We dismounted for five minutes every hour on the way back. We had to cross the Swakop just before Felseneck. The river was heavily swollen as a result of rain, and the water reached to our saddles. We got back into camp at two o'clock the next morning.

17 February 1915

My company on guard at the eight-kilometre point. Very hot. Air shimmering so much that there was little visibility. The sun was so fierce that I burned my whole face, nose and ears; my glands swelled up and I felt quite miserable for two days.

18 February 1915

Oberstleutnant Franke and his staff came for an inspection.

20 February 1915

Reconnaissance at the eight-kilometre point. We were kept busy the whole day, enemy troops in squadron formation riding up to about

---

[70] Probably Sgt Friedrich Adomeit (1887-1918) who died while a prisoner of war and is buried at the cemetery at Aus near Karas.

eight hundred metres away. A great deal of activity in Swakopmund, trains going up to the four kilometre point, troops massing in Swakopmund etc. On returning to the camp I reported my observations, and gave my opinion that any day now we would face a more significant attack.

The following day the watch officer brought identical reports, so on the morning of 23 February the entire company (112 men) marched to kilometre eleven of the Otavi Railway line.

24 February 1915

At 5.30 in the morning, we encountered large groups of enemy troops, at least eight hundred mounted riders, who had appeared to our rear and on the right flank. We galloped down to the Swakop and met Hundsdörfer, who reported that Nonidas was occupied and that there were more troops on the march. One company remained in position for the time being, and the rest returned to the camp to take possession of the high ground—the camp lay between parallel, fairly steep, rocky canyons.

Von Milkau's troops occupied the heights at the northern exit, about two kilometres from the camp. I stayed with my squad awaiting further orders. While the enemy was fighting against von Milkau, I was ordered to bring reinforcements to him. I galloped up a ravine, and all of a sudden there in front of us was von Milkau's company engaged with the enemy. In order to be able to see better, I stayed low and scaled a little rocky promontory with the horse; I could see small green flags waving, which were enemy troops, and we started to come under heavy fire from above.

Before my horse could slide down the steep rocks after my *Vice-Feldwebel* and the rest of my company, all the firing concentrated on me and my horse. I couldn't go any further forward through the ravine, even exploiting every possible nook and cranny of cover between there and the camp, since the enemy had already pushed forward and was beginning to advance on the camp. After a short while my company reached von Milkau's position without any losses.

In the camp itself, the reserve horses were immediately unloaded and driven together, carts and waggons prepared, ammunition loaded, provisions and paperwork piled up and doused with petrol. Six wounded men were left behind in the field hospital tent with a medical orderly and then everyone rode through the Swakop and up the other side of the river. I was riding together with two men along a path which continuously rose, running parallel to the camp. I climbed up with one trooper to where we could see down into the camp, which the British had already entered. On the other side of the ridge four British soldiers came up, seemingly as curious as I was. We shot them with ease, and then rode away in a cloud of dust until we rejoined the rest of the company.

Scultetus rode with one of the companies to see if Rössing was occupied, I had orders to take all the loose animals and waggons to Arandis (near the sixty-kilometre point on the Otavi railway). We saw signs of enemy troops in the river bed, so we went out into the bush, but there were enemy soldiers there as well; so we compromised by staying within twenty kilometres of the river bed.

The horses became weak; as soon as we stopped, the animals lay down, and the only way to make them stand again was to ride in between them. I had only six men with me. It was an appallingly hot day, and we had been riding since two o'clock in the morning. At five o'clock in the afternoon we finally met at Arandis railway station, quite broken and half-dead from thirst, and gradually the other sections and squads of the company trickled in.

A train from Usakos brought us food and water, for we had brought no provisions with us, and had had nothing to eat or drink since two o'clock that morning. All of us were on high alert, and twice the alarm was raised overnight, just as we had wrapped ourselves in horse-blankets and fallen asleep in a corner. False alarm both times.

23 February 1915

We occupied the *Arandiskuppe*. Railway engineers from Usakos began to dismantle the line, and we moved the camp three kilometres east of the *Arandiskuppe*.

25 February 1915

During his inspection of the camp, *Major* Wehle ordered us to move it twelve kilometres east, beyond railway kilometre seventy-four. A mounted train must always go ahead to cover the dismantling of the railway. As we learned later, on 23 February we had been attacked by a hostile force of 5,000 men, under the personal direction of General Botha, and thrown out of our camp near Felseneck. We, on the other hand, were only a company of 112 rifles, and we lost only a patrol of three men, who were captured unharmed.

1 March 1915

I received news of a transfer to *Major* Wehle's staff in Kubas as ordnance officer.

2 March 1915

I rode with a few men to Arandis and from there by railway trolley to Khangrube (which was abandoned) to bring provisions and other useful kit. At 6 o'clock in the evening I was back again in the camp with some loot.

4 March 1915

Leutnant von Könitz[71] arrived to replace me, with whom I had been exchanged from the staff.

5 March 1915

At three o'clock I rode out with my natives and my belongings, which formed just a small bundle on the second horse, and arrived at Treckkoppje railway station at seven that night. I ate with the local stationmaster and stayed there overnight.

---

[71] Probably Heinrich Freiherr von Könitz.

6 March 1915

At six in the morning I carried on through Stinkbank and Old Tsawisis to Ubib. Got to Dixon's farm at ten, off-saddled and as it was such a hot day, stayed until three o'clock in the afternoon. Reached Kubas at five.

7 and 8 March 1915

Introduction to staff officer's duties.

9 March 1915

Left at five o'clock in the morning, just me and my natives on a long patrol, seeking out water and pasture conditions in the local countryside and checking whether enemy troops are close by. I rode over Ubib, then turned north from the crossroads towards Old Tsawisis, (Farmer Dietz), from there southwards to New Tsawisis, from there across the railway at the 124-kilometer point to Aukas station. From there across the river and past the Henderson copper mine to Klein-Aukas. There I met my old friend and former colleague at the *DKG*, Richard Schettler, and stayed with him overnight.

10 March 1915

At five o'clock in the morning I rode back from there and arrived at Kubas at 11am. A total of 137 kilometers.

12 March 1915

Went with *Major* Wehle by train to Karibib. We were there all afternoon and the following day.

13 March 1915

Many errands for the staff, reports and telegrams to headquarters, supplies for the troops, and at four o'clock in the afternoon back again by train to Kubas. I am to be in charge of railways, looking after all traffic and transportation.

14 and 15 March 1915

Signficant troop movements taking place to new positions, and all of them are passing through Kubas, so there has to be a regular service from early morning to late.

15 March 1915

Orders from headquarters that the staff has to move to Jakalswater. At two o'clock in the afternoon we departed by train, and finally got to Jakalswater at seven o'clock in the in the evening after all the usual incidents, a carriage derailment, etc.

16 March 1915

The various troops came to the new positions. In the afternoon, the commander arrived and inspected our new location with *Major* Wende, departing in the evening.

17 March 1915

Alarm sounded at three in the morning, but nothing to see from the enemy.

19 March 1915

Great alarm, an enemy squadron attacked our outposts and one of our patrols, *Major* Wehle rode away alone into the bush, and no one knows where he is. Reports from scouts from which we believe the enemy is planning a major attack for tomorrow.

Wehle's positions:

At Jakalswater: the staff and artillery staff under *Hauptmann* Trainer;[72]

At Modderfontein: an artillery battery under *Hauptmann* von Münstermann, and a mounted company.

---

[72] Georg Trainer; an artillery officer, he was present at the Naulila incident on the Angolan border in 1914.

At Riet: a mounted company under *Hauptmann* von Watter,[73] an infantry company under Reserve *Hauptmann* Ohlenschlager,[74] and an artillery battery under *Hauptmann* Haüding.

At Pforte: a mounted company under *Hauptmann* Weiss and half an artillery battery under *Oberleutnant* von Weiher.[75]

In the absence of orders, I immediately had the railway trains in Jakalswater loaded with all supplies and provisions, munitions, and reserve ammunition, so as to be able to evacuate the trains immediately after a sudden attack. Major Wehle was finally back at noon, claiming that there was no prospect of a further attack from the enemy. He was dissatisfied with my actions, and ordered everything to be unloaded again. Since we, the other officers, did not share his view, I had a quiet word with *Hauptmann* Trainer; I then gave the impression of carrying out the orders, but surreptitiously allowed the most heavily loaded train to leave.

20 March 1915

At half-past four in the morning a platoon arrived by train, 30 men, the last of the *Landwehr* Corps, under Reserve *Oberleutnant* Steffen. After a short halt, our sentries joined them and they were sent as reinforcements for the command post against further attacks. The *Major*'s adjutant, *Oberleutnant* Neuhaus, went with them to deploy the troops into the correct positions.

At six o'clock in the morning, two companies of enemy troops attacked the station building from about two hundred metres away. They occupied a rocky outcrop which lay like a whale's back, about sixty metres high and 150 metres long, and opened fire. At Jakalswater we had only thirty-seven men in total, including seven officers and the railway staff. We immediately opened fire from the railway

---

[73] Wilhelm von Watter (1880-1915), a German nobleman who died from wounds sustained at Trekkopje.

[74] Dr Gustav Ohlenschlager (1867-1915), who was in civilian life a lawyer from Omaruru and mayor of Swakopmund.

[75] Hans von Weiher (1885-1915), killed that day and buried in Swakopmund.

embankment, which was at right angles to the railway buildings and lay opposite the enemy's position, and as the enemy was very well pinned down, a mutual deadly fire began. To our right on a piece of higher ground, about eight hundred metres away, appeared thirteen enemy squads simultaneously. Two of them rode out straight away, and destroyed the railway line and telegraph to our rear; we had to expect an assault from the rest at any second, of course, but as they seemed to be unclear about our strength, no attack took place.

In order to have a better view, I crawled further to the right along the railway embankment, but as soon as I raised my head to look out, a bullet grazed the left side of my head. For a moment it knocked me senseless, then I went back to my former position and heard *Major* Wehle call for me. Of course, I could not understand what he wanted over the noise of gunfire, and after two repeated queries he shouted 'Well, come over here, then.'

This was a pretty ticklish call, because he was standing at the station building and I had about to traverse about sixty metres under enemy fire across an entirely open area. I told myself: if you run, you become a battle casualty. If you don't run, you end up being court-martialled for disobedience or maybe even cowardice. You might as well run.

I had gone barely ten steps when I got a shot through the left buttock, a decent, deep flesh-wound, about eight centimetres long, and I bled like a stuck pig. The order I received from Wehle was so unnecessary and was so definitely not worth the wound I had received, that in a fury I retreated back to safety, threw myself down at the top of the railway embankment and smoked a cigarette before I started shooting again. Now came von Münstermann's battery galloping up into position immediately, and opened fire on the whale's back. I crawled to the battery, pointed out the squads deployed on our right and the two behind us, whereupon two guns fired shrapnel shells at them and all thirteen squads rode off at the gallop.

The artillery on the whale's back did not seem to be well-judged, and we saw how it was gradually abandoned. The troops had to run because for the most part we had shot down their horses, which were tied up at the foot of the rock. When only a faint fire came from that direction, *Hauptmann* Vorbeck and I advanced with two men towards the whale's back. As we approached the rock, a great number of enemy soldiers with raised hands suddenly appeared out of the outcrops and we captured forty-two, including two Boer officers. The group immediately had to throw down their rifles, ammunition belts and side-arms; Vorbeck left me and my two men alone them and went behind the rocks, and after a short time returned with a further six men, an army doctor, and fifty saddled horses. The whale's back was cleared.

The fight was over and we brought the prisoners and horses to the station. It wasn't until half-past eleven that I could get hold of our medical officer and get my wound dressed. My railway duties started again: everything that was still there had to be loaded, the prisoners put on a train, and the tracks behind us were soon repaired.

At Riet an attack had also been repulsed, and the enemy had retreated, but as another attack was expected the following morning, and our position there was too weak, the troops were ordered to return to Kubas. Some 4,000 to 5,000 enemy mounted troops had attacked Pforte, and the entire garrison was captured, with several killed or wounded including von Weiher, the dashing officer in charge of the artillery battery. At four o'clock in the afternoon, *Major* Wehle ordered a retreat from Jakalswater to Dorstrevier railway station. He gave me orders to escort the fifty captured horses, but at walking pace so that he could reach me at any moment. (*Oberleutnant* Neuhaus, the adjutant, had been taken prisoner at Pforte, so I was now adjutant and ordnance officer.) I only had two men to help with the transport of the horses, so I took six of the prisoners off the railway train and brought them along; each one was coupled to a string of eight horses, so they couldn't make off from me.

My bandage did not stop me riding. The wound burned, and I was aching terribly; my leg gradually became so stiff that at every stop one of my men had to lift my leg over the saddle. Six hours riding at a walk is not one of my most beautiful war memories. At ten o'clock in the evening we reached Dorstrevier station, dead-tired, hungry, and parched. The captured, wounded and dead were immediately transported by train to Karibib. Finally by about half-past midnight I was done in. I found a spot on a pile of kitbags in a railway waggon, rolled myself in my coat and did not need a lullaby to fall asleep.

After approximately half an hour's slumber I realised that the train was in motion. But *I* was in charge of the railway... so who had given the order to leave? I clambered from waggon to waggon until I reached the engine, and learned from the train driver that *Major* Wehle had ordered him to drive the train to Kubas immediately. Why and for what reason? Incomprehensible, but classic Wehle: do this one minute, do that the next!

In Kubas my former *DKG* colleague Otto Meyer fortified me with a bite to eat and some schnapps, and I took a locomotive back to Dorstrevier, where I arrived at five o'clock in the morning. I had been looking forward to some decent sleep, but it became sheer hell because there was so much to do. Reports and encrypted telegrams to headquarters; personnel re-assignments and so on. My wound, which was seriously inflamed by the long ride, had to be treated again and re-dressed and the doctor forbade me to ride any further. Scarcely ten minutes later, Wehle ordered me to ride to Kubas and to make sure that all the available railway locomotives were to go to Dorstrevier. When I told him the doctor had banned me from riding, Wehle said 'Oh, you'll be fine if you take it slowly.' I was in agony, but what can you do? An order is an order, so I rode with my natives. I had gone barely three kilometres when a locomotive from Kubas appeared. I gave my boy my two horses to ride with slowly to Kubas, halted the locomotive and let it take me back to Kubas. In the afternoon the rest of the staff and the other troops gradually arrived in Kubas.

22 to 27 of March was very busy with railway transport, the various troops units being ordered to new positions, telephone and telegraph going incessantly, we cleared out Kubas and packed up; our staff quarters were constantly changing: retreating all the time. As a result I had to set out new transport routes; water had to be stored for the railway in huge tanks; I had to provide feed and water for the horses and sort out water for the individual companies and so on. All of these tasks now fell to me instead of the captured adjutant.

On 24 March I received a telegram from Windhoek to say that our son Heinz had been born. Emmy was transferred from Karibib to Windhoek before the birth, so as to be in the hands of our good Dr. Brenner. The following day news of the battle and our losses and injuries reached Windhoek, causing my poor wife the most awful worry until—two days later—she received my written report of the nature of my injury.

On 28 March, *Major* Ritter took command over the whole division. *Major* Wehle was transferred to Otjiwarongo district and later Tsumeb. That suited him better because he was really no strategist, and the battle at Jakalswater should not have ended as it did.

Wehle left on 29 March, and we were not sad to see him go. He had everything loaded onto his waggon including provisions that actually belonged to the staff, so *Oberleutnant* Fricke, and I secretly raided the waggon and took everything we needed, together with some special delicacies he had ordered and reserved for himself.

The whole *Schutztruppe* was now divided into two equal parts, one under the command of *Major* Ritter, the other under *Major* Bauszus.[76] I stayed on Ritter's staff. I had known Ritter since 1901, when he was a lieutenant in the *Schutztruppe*, and I had spent some splendid days with him in Lüderitzbucht and on a trip to Keetmanshoop. In 1904 I was involved with him (then *Oberleutnant*) in two big battles in the Herero war, so we were very friendly. He was a magnificent officer and a real daredevil. I was no longer adjutant, thank God, as Ritter had *Oberleutnant* von Geldern as adjutant.

The main staff were based in Ababis, while three of us stayed at the front as orderly officers and did our daily duties. Every morning all units were on high alert until eight o'clock, as we expected an attack to come, but the enemy had probably suffered losses at Jakalswater and left us in peace. My injuries did not heal, since I did not have the rest I needed. A giant abscess had formed at the head-wound, which the doctor opened twice while I knelt under some trees (we had no field

---

[76] Hans Bauszus (1871-1955). An enthusiastic Nazi, he became an *SS-Brigadeführer* in the 1930s.

hospital). In addition, a length of about three centimetres on my thigh did not close up.

I refused to go to the hospital because I was afraid they would transfer me back to base and away from the front. At the doctor's request, *Major* Ritter ordered me to go to Karibib hospital on 12 April, and promised me that I would definitely return to him afterwards. In Karibib, Dr. Friedrich removed the big abscess by cutting deeply into it, but he had to operate under anaesthetic on a second abscess, which had formed on my neck and was not inclined to heal. Since the other wound on my thigh did not want to close, Dr. Friedrich cut it open again at my request, and found in it a two-inch-long piece of my riding-trousers. The cloth had been embedded by the shot and was not discovered when the wound was first dressed. The wound healed within a few days.

As the British continued to advance, Karibib was partly evacuated and the wounded transported to the hospital at Otjiwarongo.

On 30 April I left with *Oberleutnant* (pilot) Fiedler,[77] who had crashed in Karibib and had a hole in his skull (we had only two very old planes, both of which were soon wrecks). We were sitting on the front platform of a railway carriage (the carriages were filled with sick and wounded men evacuated from Karibib), and after many interruptions, breakdowns of the locomotives, etc., we arrived at Otjiwarongo after travelling for a fortnight.

We were not admitted to the hospital because it was full, and I soon found myself under a tree, where the termites almost ate me alive at night. Sometimes on a bench on a stoep; sometimes in a workshop on cartridge boxes; and once in the opulent bed of the commander—he was not there—until Director Hörleinof the German Diamond Co. of the German Diamond Company built a small corrugated iron building about three hundred metres from the hospital. I went to the hospital every morning, and since there was a different doctor on duty each day, and each doctor always prescribed precisely the opposite of the

---

[77] The Austrian pilot Paul Fiedler (1884-1955) crashed his Roland biplane on 17 April 1915. He returned to South-West Africa after the war to manage a farm.

treatment of his predecessor, there was no prospect of the wound healing.

On 5 May the British occupied Karibib, and on May 7, Okahandja.

Colonel Grant, who was taken prisoner at Sandfontein on 27 September 1914, was interned at Waterberg. He had to be sent to Tsumeb, and although I had no duties because I was on sick leave, the commander requested that I escort him. We went by train to Tsumeb on 10 May, and I was back in Otjiwarongo the following day.

Thirty-nine captured English officers arrived at Otjiwarongo en route to Namutoni on 19 May. I had to act as an interpreter and provide for their accommodation and guards overnight.

On 20 May the Governor, Dr Seitz, *Oberstleutnant* Franke, *Hauptmann* Trainer and an officer acting as an interpreter went by train to Giftkuppe for negotiations there with General Botha for a possible end to hostilities. Treaties collapsed and the conflict continued.

I was fed up with life in Otjiwarongo and tired of the doctoring there, so when my wound was only partially healed I tricked the senior doctor into signing me off as healthy. On 24 May I reported to the local commander, and travelled back by train to Ritter, who now had his headquarters in Kalkfeld, with the troops belonging to the division deployed all around Kalkfeld. *Oberleutnant* von Geldern was adjutant; Fricke, von Loßnitzer,[78] and I were ordnance officers; *Vice-Feldwebel* Görgens[79] and Hümann[80] (head surveyor of Windhoek) were local guides; as well as two *Unteroffiziere* and six men.

June was a state of constant alert. I was working on the railway service day and night as trains arrived or were deployed elsewhere. The weather was unpleasant: so cold that in the mornings the horses'

---

[78] Erich von Loßnitzer (1886-1942) became one of the leaders of the Nazi party in South-West Africa in the 1930s before being deported to Germany.

[79] Görgens was district officer for Omaruru and director of surveys of German South-West Africa.

[80] Frans Hümann succeeded Görgens as director of surveys of German South-West Africa in 1912.

drinking-troughs were frozen. I spent three days with two men on patrol in the Erongo mountains when enemy aeroplanes appeared over Kalkfeld, and therefore all the trains had to be driven into the emergency sidings in dense bush at night.

On 29 May *Oberleutnant* Scheele[81] was intending to fly to Omaruru to throw some bombs at the enemy camp. But he crashed when the engine failed shortly after take-off. Major Ritter and I were about twenty metres away watching him take-off, and we pulled him out of the burning aeroplane with a broken leg and broken nose.

On 19 June the enemy occupied Omaruru, and on the same night, Epako. *Leutnant* von Dewitz was wounded there, captured and taken away. There was a danger of them coming to Kalkfeld and encircling us, so we evacuated and at seven o'clock in the morning on 21 June Ritter's entire command set off: three batteries and two mounted companies, baggage and staff (three companies providing rear-guard cover behind us).

It was a terrible march. Usually marching only in step, because the heavily loaded munition and provision waggons proceeded slowly in the deep sand, all pulled by mules because we didn't have any motor vehicles. We stopped for the night at six that evening. We set out the next day at eight o'clock in the morning for a long march. At eleven o'clock we arrived at Erundu, and after giving the animals food and water we continued on a very bad road until eleven o'clock that night. We blew up the bridge at Erundu.

On 23 June we were in an area that provided good grazing for the animals, and by nine in the morning we had reached only point 27-3 of the Otavi railway. We remained there until 24 June. We led the animals to the water station at Otjitazu, and at four in the afternoon we rode through Otjiwarongo. We carried on until nine o'clock in the evening, and then bivouacked for the night.

We had a long march on 25 June, starting at seven o'clock, to kilometre 402 of the Otavi railway, where I had ordered a water train. It took a long time for all the animals to drink. There was news that the

---

[81] Alexander von Scheele (1894-1942), German military aviation pioneer.

enemy is attacking from all sides and has occupied Waterberg, so the three rearguard companies were quickly called in, arriving at two o'clock in the afternoon. At four o'clock we had a long march until ten o'clock that night, and then took a break overnight in dense bush. We started again at seven on the morning of 26 June, and were at Okaputa by nine. I rode ahead with *Major* Ritter, to the farms of de Jong and V. Erpf,[82] and fed and watered the animals there in a large maize field. We had to abandon the farm, destroying the pumps and water systems to render them useless to the enemy, and then marched until nine o'clock in the evening.

On 27 June we left at seven in the morning and went on until Komukanti, there we watered again from a previously-arranged water train, and continue until ten that evening, where we stayed at kilometre 488 of the Otavi railway for the night.

We set of at seven in the morning on 28 June and arrived in Otavifontein at 8.30am. The local commander Reserve *Hauptmann* Ohlenschlager, who knew the troops were on their way, had not prepared anything and was seriously chewed out for it by Major Ritter. At nine o'clock the commander arrived in a motor-car with *Hauptmann* Trainer, and although Ritter showed him his excellent defence position at Otavifontein, he ordered that the entire company go back down the Otjenga road for three kilometres and take up position at the *Eisenpforte*.

This was the wrong place. If we had followed Ritter's plan it would probably not have been possible for the British to take Otavifontein. We later heard from them that it would have been a catastrophe for their men, as a retreat to the nearest water station (unlike us, they were not able to arrange transport of water by railway) would have caused the loss of most of their horses. On Franke's orders our whole company was torn apart: the three batteries were placed individually on various hillocks, the companies stationed around without any organised structure, and the staff remained in the centre.

---

[82] Okaputa is still owned by the Erpf family.

On 29 June I went on foot as close as I possibly could to Otavifontein to get water barrels: we could not lead the horses out of the emplacements to drink because of the proximity of the enemy. Two enemy planes flew over Otavi and Otavifontein for an hour-and-a-half, they threw five bombs but did not cause any damage.

During the evening of 30 June news came at seven o'clock that Okaputa was occupied by the enemy, and there was heavy artillery on the march. Everyone on high alert.

At seven in the morning on 1 July the enemy shot at our outposts. The general staff rode out to Otavifontein at seven o'clock; they had been standing all night with saddled horses, and could signal using lights to the batteries and companies. Aeroplanes appeared again and we shot at them. We rode up to a big field of maize below the native location; the Second Reserve and Fifth Field Company were already in combat between the maize field and Otavi, with enemy artillery firing over us. I was ordered to take command of Number Three Battery and the Third Reserve Company, which had not yet arrived, and to direct them into new positions. I dashed at a wild gallop under the most violent fire (every ordnance officer has to have an escort in the battle, who must ride just behind him, and if the officer falls, the escort will have to carry on the message). I wasn't hit, but my poor *Unteroffizier* escort was brought down after a bullet struck his horse.

After 30 minutes I reached the batteries and the company and directed them into the positions as ordered. Then at the gallop back to the staff. When I got there, the two companies had not been able to hold their positions and had fallen back, and the staff had also retreated back until I found them at the railway station at the entrance to Otavi Gorge. In the meantime the enemy had reached Otavi; incomprehensibly, two of Bauszus' companies lying in position at Sargberg (ten kilometres north of us) had been pulled back, leaving the enemy free to approach our left flank.

Our companies headed right, towards Gauss. At the entrance to the ravine, a *Zahlmeister* came towards us, badly wounded, and reported that both sides of the gorge were occupied by the enemy; and that his two carts, transporting uniforms and men, had been hit. According to

Hümann, the surveyor, the only way out for the staff officers was to the right, towards the mountain; but *Major* Ritter suddenly dug his spurs into his horse's side and flew into the ravine, over the fallen men and horses lying there. I could only see how the staff were galloping to the right (I was directly behind Ritter) but since I was always told that you should stay with the commanding officer, I raced behind him, about two horse-lengths behind. Head down on the horse's neck as it galloped through deadly firing from each side; towards the end of the ravine, which is about half a kilometre long, the firing eased and we slowed down our horses. We were alone without our men. Ritter's horse was shot through the withers and had to be destroyed that evening, I had a shot through the front pocket of my rucksack; I kept as a souvenir the perforated card that was in it.

After about two hundred metres we came across our three batteries, which had taken up position at entirely the wrong locations and had not come under fire at all. The batteries and the gradually growing companies continued marching up to the previously planned rendezvous point. As there was no action against us from the enemy, we carried on marching during the night to Bauszus' camp at Sargberg. I had orders to hand over the batteries, and when I returned in the dark to the place where the staff had grouped, the latter had already disappeared. I looked everywhere and there was nothing visible, just the faint noise from the troops ahead during the last five kilometres of my search of the road. At two o'clock in the morning, I still had not found the rest of the staff, but I was done in—having been riding since seven that morning and no sleep the night before. I was dead-tired; after I saddled my horse and gave it some food, I wrapped a rug around myself and dossed down beside the horse.

By 2 July the enemy had not attacked us again. The Union troops did not seem intent on following up the battle with further action, but there were reports from the north that the enemy had bypassed our position, already occupying Outjo and almost in Okaukuejo.

On 3 July the reports from the day before were confirmed, and that Third Reserve Company had arrived in Gauss.

On 4 July came orders from the command, the entire force was to go to Khorab and take up a defensive position there. Khorab is a farm with a large farmhouse, good water and lots of it. We set off marching at six o'clock in the evening (marching at night as the dust clouds betray our movements to the enemy in the daytime). Horribly bad road, slow progress. The baggage carts were often coming to a halt; to determine the cause I had to ride alongside the road, and ended up in a hole with my horse three times in one night. We got to Khorab at midnight, and spent the night where we stood.

On 5 July the two companies now set up a circular defensive position around the farmhouse and water station, with Bauszus' men defending the northern half and our men facing south towards Otavifontein. Everyone was constantly on alert, day and night. In order to prevent further unpleasant fighting and bloodshed (but probably because the Boers showed reluctance to continue the struggle) General Botha offered peace negotiations. For ourselves, the situation was such that our troops had not yet been defeated, but we were hemmed in on all sides; our artillery no longer possessed ammunition; there were not enough shells for a battle; we had no feed for the horses; and we had nothing to eat except meat.

On 6 July, from seven o'clock in the morning, a cease-fire was agreed and the governor and military commander, together with their staff, arranged for talks and negotiations with Botha. These negotiations continued until 8 July, when Botha entered upon the most essential points of our conditions. Troops on active service were to be interned at Aus in the south of the country. Reservists were to be released, and they could return to their homes and farms and resume their employment. All war material and government property was to be confiscated by the enemy, private property was not to be touched. Botha wanted to express his appreciation to the officers by allowing them to keep their horses and weapons as personal property.

This surrender was signed by both sides on 9 July 1915. When Botha got the lists of names showing over 2,200 men he said he had been tricked, because he knew that we had 15,000 men. Franke replied,

"If we had 15,000 men, then you wouldn't be here and we wouldn't be in this position."

From 10 to 14 July, the reservists were gradually removed by train. All officers remained behind; we had to affirm that in this war we would no longer fight against the Union and England, which of course we did without hesitation or remorse—for there was no way for us to get out of the country, and we had no troops in the country. On 15 July we finally got our passes and decided to return to our homes, as the railroad was too chaotic and we did not want to leave our horses behind.

The English lent us one of own army wagons with six mules, which we had to leave at Omaruru. At half-past three in the afternoon we rode: *Leutnant* Kundt, Dr. Gumprecht[83] and I, Dr. Günther the veterinary officer and Görgens the director of surveys, with our five servants. At seven o'clock we went unchecked through Otavifontein, which was occupied by a large number of English troops, and camped for the night about 8 kilometres further south.

On 16 July we continued at seven o'clock in the morning. At nine we were in Otjikurumane, where we stopped to drink, farmhouse and everything destroyed. As it was very hot, we off-saddled at eleven o'clock for lunch. Before our departure from Khorab, I had shot a fat ox for the staff (it had already been claimed by the English) and had a haunch of beef on the wagon. At three o'clock we moved on, passed Gaidaus an hour later, until setting camp at nine that night.

We set off at six on the morning of 17 July: we came on a large group of Boer troops marching and firing their guns off apparently just for fun, so that we were glad to get through their lines safely. We stopped for water at Otjenga at ten o'clock and then stayed in good pasture for the animals from midday to four in the afternoon. From Khorab to Otjenga is 110 kilometres. In the afternoon we took the road to Owumerume until ten o'clock at night and then stopped for the night.

We left at six in the morning on 18 July. Two hours later we turned off our path to the outpost Onjunbombupa on Okosongomingo

---

[83] Probably Dr . W. Gumprecht, who was a lawyer in Swakopmund.

farm[84] (Schneider) where we arrived at eleven o'clock, 50 kilometres from Otjenga. We had good water and pasture there, and got some food for our animals. Since we had to rest, we stayed here until the following morning. We bought ourselves a small calf, which was slaughtered and added to our provisions.

19 July: we were away at six o'clock, riding cross-country to Osonjahe; and since we did not find any water there, twenty kilometres further to the farm Hohenfels where *Graf* von Bentheim[85] and his wife entertained us with coffee and *vetkoek*. At six o'clock we rode off cross-country, missed our path (to which local natives finally directed us) and set camp for the night at eleven o'clock.

We left on 20 July at six in the morning and went thirty-four kilometres via Omusewa Nari, thirty-four kilometres to Ovitue (*Major* Chogo), where we arrived at ten o'clock. We stopped about three hundred metres before the farm to make ourselves presentable, and even shaved, before visiting the Chogo family, who invited us to lunch. At three o'clock we rode on, passed Ehameno after seventeen kilometres and went on another eight kilometres before setting camp for the night.

July 21: Departure eight o'clock in the morning, past Osongutu farm and after another twenty-seven kilometres we had a midday break until three o'clock. Then another twenty-two kilometres. Stopped at Okaturua farm, where we watered the animals, then on until seven o'clock in the evening.

On 22 July we set out at six o'clock and reached the farm Okatete after eighteen kilometers. We drank, and then off-saddled at ten o'clock, five kilometres further in good pasture. At three o'clock we went on to Omburu farm (owned by von Prittwitz[86]) where everything was destroyed; von Prittwitz served with us as an officer. Six kilometres

---

[84] Still owned by the Schneider family, now part of the Waterberg conservancy.
[85] Richard *Graf* zu Bentheim-Tecklenburg-Rheda (1840-1921), a German nobleman who retired to South-West Africa after a career in the East Indies.
[86] Probably Joachim von Prittwitz (1876-1952), whose son was later mayor of Swakopmund.

further to the farm Waldfrieden (farmer Hecht[87]). Hecht looked after us very nicely. We left our horses and saddles there until we could retrieve them when we were back in our own homes, and stayed there overnight.

On 23 July we all drove with the waggon to Omaruru. We were at Märtins[88] for breakfast, and after we had returned our waggon and span of mules to the English authorities, we set off to Karibib by train at three o'clock. There we parted, each one of us travelling to his home. Only Dr. Gumprecht and I had to go to Windhoek, where our families were at the time. That evening and overnight we were guests of Gustav Rösemann.[89]

On 24 July 1915, at 7.30am, our train left for Windhoek. We were lying on food sacks on an open wagon, with no luggage apart from a rifle, and finally reached Windhoek at six o'clock in the evening, received with joy by our wives and children. My second son Heinz was just four months old when I saw him for the first time. We celebrated our reunion at a splendid supper, such as we had not enjoyed for a year. I also rediscovered civilian clothes, and discarded a rather ragged military uniform after reporting to the English authorities. The war was over for us. It was not really a glorious victory for the British, but the Union had invested no fewer than 85,000 men against a group of about 2,400 men, including all reserves and regular troops. It was the game of one mouse against many cats.

We all needed and wanted to go back to our places of residence: for us, Swakopmund. But the departure was shifted from day to day, no trains were available, and the English used every possible excuse. It appeared that in Swakopmund the authorities had not yet finished with the stealing and transport of private property. After about twelve days we were eventually 'loaded'. We came with two children; Dr. Brenner, with wife, sister-in-law, and two children; and August Schulze[90] with

---

[87] Probably Ernst Hecht.

[88] W. Märtins had a restaurant at Nonidas and may have provided refreshments at other railway stations near Swakopund.

[89] The hotel that Rösemann built is still standing in Karibib.

[90] Schulze ran an advertising bureau.

wife, sister-in-law, and four children. Sixteen of us in a closed freight car, used for transporting cattle, which had not yet been cleaned, and so we travelled over three days and three nights (the usual travel time being twelve hours) to Swakopmund.

Our house looked awful. Anything which was not riveted or nailed down had been stolen or smashed; most of the furniture destroyed and taken, or carted off to other houses, where we discovered it again, piece by piece. Everything was chaotic and filthy. In the kitchen (our house had served as the medical officers' mess!) there was a pile of food and other refuse in a corner a metre high; and we spent three days clearing it out with shovels.

Little by little, we were able to restore the house to a habitable state, but everything dear to us and irreplaceable such as our wedding gifts, silver, crystal, porcelain, our extensive library, my diaries; all sacked and stolen. What the looters could not or would not take with them, they smashed and destroyed, discarding the debris in the backyard.

DIETRICH REIMER (ERNST VOHSEN), BERLIN SW 48.

Figure 4. The certificate for Mansfeld's Iron Cross award.

Gradually our former employees returned to us from all over the place, but business premises were just as bad: entire warehouses cleared of their contents; pieces of office furniture missing and pianos and harmoniums installed in their place. It was weeks before we could resume our business. Active hostilities and fighting had, of course, ended, but the war had not finished for us. Even though we were at liberty, we were under the rule of a foreign enemy: prisoners of war who had nothing to say.

We had to rebuild. Commercial contact with the homeland was forbidden, under heavy penalty, so we could not get money, support or advice from Berlin. We did not have the emergency money created by the German government during the war, the so-called *Seitzscheine*. This was declared worthless and not recognized by the Union government; only the British pound sterling could be used for payment. We therefore had to borrow credit from the English banks that immediately came into the colony. They awarded credit at first only against mortgages on property. As the owner of the whole of the land of Swakopmund and Lüderitzbucht we fought a tough battle with the British authorities, who had taken over large tracts of our property because of our mineral rights and our mines.

Food and all other commodities, clothing and spirits were imported from Cape Town, and gradually a lively trade unfolded. There was no milk, so at my request Dr. Hartig of the Liebig Company in Heusis sent a cow and calf in order that we could supply milk to our two children (Heinz was only six months old). The cow was almost out of milk but we had a second cow, which calved, and through good feeding with lucerne, maize and mash from the brewery the milk yield finally increased so that we could give it to our neighbours.

In 1916, Werner fell ill with a severe pulmonary inflammation, and he was still getting malaria, which he had picked up during his stay in Windhoek. Once he was better, Emmy took him and Heinz to convalesce in Klein-Windhoek for six weeks.

In 1917 Emmy and I spent two weeks as guests of our friend Venuleth on his farm Okanjati near Otjiwarongo, we had a wonderful time there.

In 1918 influenza, a terrible lung disease, swept through a large number of white populations. The disease was very severe in Swakopmund, too. Emmy and Werner were very ill for a long time, Heinz and I were spared. All the natives caught it. They sickened and died like flies and were buried in mass graves at night; and of course that meant that there were no native staff at all in the house throughout that terrible time. Of all the Company staff there were only three healthy employees, apart from me, and all business activity came to a standstill.

On 20 June 1919, on the day of the peace,[91] our Herbert was born. Peace! But what a peace for us Germans and for our South-West Africa; because our beautiful country that we cherished and held dear, for which we had worked and fought, no longer belonged to us and became the mandate of the Union government. The German *Schutztruppe*, now interned in Aus, was transported to Germany, and all those who were not acceptable to the new government were expelled and repatriated by the civilian administration. They were expelled with unbelievable brutality, often with just an hour's notice, and transported by ship in the harshest way possible. I know of hundreds of examples, enough to fill a book by themselves.

Despite the position I held, we were not expelled; for that I am indebted to a magistrate, as he told me that the government needed me and Dr. Reuning to manage the possessions of the Company.

In order to secure their possessions, all of the large and small diamond companies decided to unite into a single huge organisation. For this purpose, Dr. Lübbert,[92] a lawyer from Lüderitzbucht, travelled to Germany with a full power of attorney under English law. I will not explain why this German company did not come about, and what the

---

[91] On this day the German cabinet resigned en masse over whether or not to accept the terms of the Treaty of Versailles.
[92] Erich Lübbert (1883-1963).

view and mood was in the protected area;[93] but Dr. Lübbert sold the entire South-West African diamond industry to an English company, the Consolidated Diamond Company,[94] and earned enough commission to make his fortune. Possession of the diamond fields was thus under the control of the English government, but the land ownership and the mining rights of the *DKG* remained a thorn in their flesh; the English did not want to recognise our rights, and opposed them, although these rights had repeatedly been verified and confirmed by the German government.

The government therefore set up a so-called Concession Commission, consisting of three judges and a large staff of secretaries and stenographers, who argued during six weeks of preliminary preparation, and thereafter for six weeks, until the case was decided in our favour. Dr Reuning and I, with the support of three lawyers, spent twelve weeks working inhuman hours late into the night; dredging up witnesses, ancient court cases, and so on in order to overcome the most rarefied objections of the Commission. While this work was going on I had the bad luck to dislocate my right arm one Sunday morning while riding, when my horse fell while jumping a fence. It was strapped up tightly for three weeks, which caused me great discomfort.

The head office in Berlin was contacted by a Cape Town consortium in connection with the sale of our entire land and mine rights, in order to avoid more chicanery from the Mandate government—and potential expropriation. Finally, at the end of 1920, after four weeks' negotiations in Cape Town, our Director Bredow from Berlin and I completed the sale to the South-West Finance Corporation. The company retained only its commercial center in Swakopmund, with its Tsumeb branch and its plots of land. Berlin had decided to maintain these business at my instigation, for I thought it a duty of honour that the Company—as the biggest and oldest in the country, and the successor of Lüderitz, the founder of South-West Africa—did not pull out of the country altogether.

---

[93] i.e. the *Sperrgebiet*.
[94] Consolidated Diamond Mines of South-West Africa.

In March 1921 I went with Emmy on a 3 weeks holiday to Cape Town. During this time our old friend Mrs Weitzenberg[95] looked after our house and the children so well that Herbert would not go back to his mother when we returned.

With his profits from Consolidated Diamond Mines, Dr. Lübbert had bought a large stock-holding in the *DKG*. In previous court cases he had made no secret of his dislike for the Company; things came to a head; someone in Berlin did not watch him carefully enough; and he outwitted them. They sold off the rest of the Company to him, and the fate of the *DKG* was sealed. In September 1921 I returned to Germany with my family. After 22½ years, my work at the *DKG* was over.

---

[95] Perhaps the wife of Arno Weitzenberg, a former *Schutztruppe* officer who farmed ostriches near Swakopmund.

Germany

Germany

There was an influenza epidemic in Swakopmund at the time of our departure. Werner had caught it again; and although Dr. Brenner declared him to be unfit to travel, our travel arrangements could not be changed, and we could not of course leave him behind. Emmy and I took the great risk of bringing him on board tightly wrapped in blankets. His fever disappeared after three days and he completely recovered after a short while. Herbert, too, was sick, and lay apathetic in the cabin for several days. About three-quarters of the passengers suffered from influenza.

Arriving in Hamburg, first of all we had to find somewhere to live. Under the socialist government, all housing had to be allocated by the housing authority; and after many tough arguments with the office we were able to buy a furnished flat on Güntherstrasse in early 1922. Germany was in a terrible state. The post-war period had created conditions which we—expatriates, living overseas for a long time—had not imagined possible in our old homeland. This was no socialist republic: but rather communism in full bloom.

The incorruptible German official had disappeared, Jews had all the prime positions; corruption and the black market were everywhere and the phrases 'honest merchant' and 'in good faith' no longer existed. For us, who still believed in these concepts, it was a long way from our old home and not easy to adjust to life in the new, rotten environment. I openly admit that I was often ashamed to be German. German money had been totally devalued by a nonsensical inflation so that the British pound rose to be worth billions of marks. We had pounds and could live well, but of course values had also risen as a result; because what cost pennies before, now cost millions of marks. To mention only two examples: the house that we bought in the Güntherstrasse had a value of perhaps two thousand marks. And for this I had to pay sixty-five thousand marks. Emmy had to pay two million marks for some stem parsley—former value about tuppence.

153

Income-tax, employee insurance tax, tax on property and wealth all rose steadily; In addition to this, the state issued mandatory bonds which were declared as worthless after a short time. Life in Hamburg required a lot of money. I tried to do deals with export agencies, but they did not make much progress. I became involved in investing my capital with a number of larger traders, but every one of them—despite the immense caution I observed—turned out to be fraudulent enterprises, and I lost a large part of the savings I had earned in South-West Africa. It was pointless to try to take these criminals to court, because the state itself had become the greatest crook and swindler, and had made all its citizens' property (bonds, savings deposits, life insurance, industrial shares and so on) worthless through inflation. The household also spent huge sums annually, so I decided to go back to South Africa with what remained of our property at the end of 1928 in order to start again.

I arrived in Cape Town on 9 January 1929 and joined the existing liquor wholesale company Hansa Ltd with the intention of taking over the business. After a protracted period spent poring over the books, I bought the company in April 1929. In November 1929, Emmy and the three boys followed me to Cape Town. I didn't have enough available capital for Hansa Ltd, because I had to take over nonsensically large stocks of German beers in various ports, Cape Town, Port Elizabeth, East London and Durban.

Customers paid very slowly, so that there was a constant outstanding credit of £2,000 owed to the company. Customs duty and transport always necessitated more cash-flow, so I sold the debt for £600.

At the end of 1931 I was in trouble. Schriewer, the previous owner of Hansa Ltd, had ceded my remaining debt to the local building contractor, Hoheisen,[96] a very wealthy man. I had enjoyed good and

---

[96] Alfred August Hoheisen (1878-1965), prominent colonial building contractor, responsible for the Wolmarans Street synagogue in Johannesburg and Groote Schuur Medical School in Cape Town.

friendly relations until this noble gentleman refused a further deferment of the current debt for three months; demanded immediate payment, and threatened me to bankrupt me otherwise (for unknown reasons, as my balance sheet was perfectly healthy when the auditors, Hoheisen's trustee and the Board of Executors checked it).

To avoid this and to maintain the reputation of our good name, I decided to sell Hansa Ltd. As always in such a situation, I made further losses on the capital I had invested.

The next few years were the most unpleasant of my life. Previously well-off, we had to scrimp and save everywhere. I earned a little through various minor jobs until in April 1933 I became the general representative for South-West Africa for the African Life Insurance Company of Johannesburg, and went to Windhoek. For eighteen months I drove across South-West Africa for the company, and got some excellent sales figures. However, I lost this position at the end of 1934 because the company wasn't making enough profit, and I returned to Cape Town.

In February 1935 I went to work for E. Schiengemann (Pty) Ltd, where I stayed until July 1941. I was also secretary of the German Association of Cape Town Ltd, which brought me a further fifteen pounds per month, and our living conditions improved greatly.

In March 1939, our youngest son, Herbert, went to Germany to join the labour service and then to undertake his military service. After a ten-year absence Emmy travelled in June 1939 to see the old homeland once again for a few months.

Then, in September 1939, the war that nobody conceived of broke out. The war made it impossible for Emmy to return to Cape Town. It robbed us of our beloved Herbert; he died a heroic death for his fatherland on 27 May 1940, in a battle near Sedan.

Werner, who was married and held a good position in Windhoek; and Heinz (who had passed his architectural examinations in November 1939) were interned as Germans by the Union government, and I remained here on my own.

I choose to spare myself descriptions of this time since the outbreak of war. I cannot tell you about my monotonous existence, and Emmy and Werner and Heinz have had their own experiences.

I now have only one wish: that this dreadful war will soon come to an end, and our family may be reunited, so that my sons can be returned to me for the few remaining years of my life.

Emmy, the boys and I have had many beautiful years in our lives; but we have also had to endure awful times. It has truly been a 'gypsy life'.

Eugen Mansfeld
Cape Town, March 1942

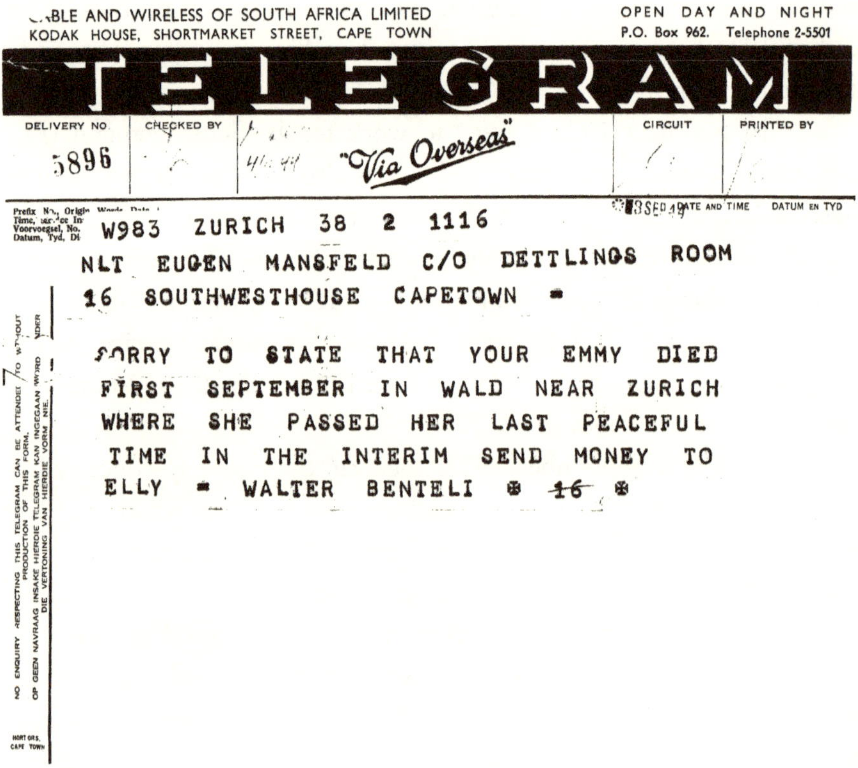

CABLE AND WIRELESS OF SOUTH AFRICA LIMITED
KODAK HOUSE, SHORTMARKET STREET, CAPE TOWN

OPEN DAY AND NIGHT
P.O. Box 962. Telephone 2-5501

TELEGRAM

"Via Overseas"

DELIVERY NO. 5896 CHECKED BY CIRCUIT PRINTED BY

W983 ZURICH 38 2 1116

NLT EUGEN MANSFELD C/O DETTLINGS ROOM
16 SOUTHWESTHOUSE CAPETOWN

SORRY TO STATE THAT YOUR EMMY DIED
FIRST SEPTEMBER IN WALD NEAR ZURICH
WHERE SHE PASSED HER LAST PEACEFUL
TIME IN THE INTERIM SEND MONEY TO
ELLY WALTER BENTELI 16

Figure 5. Telegram informing Eugen Mansfeld of his wife's death.

Postscript

Eugen Mansfeld never saw his wife Emmy again. She died in Wald near Zurich, Switzerland, on 1 September 1944. Her brother-in-law informed Eugen Mansfeld by telegram.

Herbert Mansfeld is buried in Noyers-Pont-Maugis in the Ardennes in northern France. He died on 27 May 1940, possibly as a result of wounds sustained during the German invasion of France. He was twenty years old.

Werner Mansfeld and his wife divorced following his release from internment in 1945.

Eugen Mansfeld died in Cape Town in 1954, aged 83.

The Republic of Namibia, formerly known as South-West Africa, gained independence from South Africa on 21 March 1990 following the country's first free elections. Sam Nujoma was sworn in as the country's first President.

In 2004 the German government offered its first formal apology for the colonial campaign of genocide against the Herero people between 1904 and 1907.

Glossary

Arandiskuppe	A rock formation near the settlement of Arandis
Bezirksamtmann	District officer
Deutsche Kolonial Gesellschaft für Süd West Afrika(DKG)	German Colonial South-West African Company
Distriktschef	District head
Etappenkommandant	Administrative commander
Generalstabshauptmann	Captain of the general staff
Kaiserlichen Schutztruppe für Südwest Afrika	The Imperial German Colonial Armed Force of Southwest Africa.
Landwehr	German reserve or territorial soldiers.
Schwarzen Klippen	'Black cliffs'; a cliff formation near Walvis Bay
Schützen-Füsilier-Regiment Nr. 108	108 Fusilier Regiment of the army of the kingdom of Saxony
Seitzscheine	Emergency paper currency issued in Germany during the First World War
Sperrgebiet	The 'prohibited area' given up for diamond mining
Vetkoek	Fried doughballs
Zahlmeister	Paymaster

German military ranks

Generaloberst	General
Generalleutnant	Lieutenant general
Oberst	Colonel
Oberstleutnant	Lieutenant colonel
Major	Major
Hauptmann	Captain
Flieger-Oberleutnant	Flying officer
Oberleutnant	First lieutenant
Leutnant	Second lieutenant
Feldwebel	Company sergeant major
Vice-Feldwebel	Sergeant major/senior NCO
Sergeant	Sergeant
Unteroffizer	Corporal
Reiter	Trooper
Gefreiter	Private

Bibliography

Axis History Forum, forum.axishistory.com;

Blumhagen, H., *Südafrika (unter einschluss von Südwestafrika)* (Hamburg: L. Friederichsen & Co.: 1921);

Davis, Sam, *SWA Jahrbuch 1972* (Windhoek: South-West Africa Publications (Pty) Ltd: 1972);

The Denkmal Project, www.denkmalprojekt.org;

Dierks, Dr Klaus, *The Namibia Library of Dr Klaus Dierks*, www.klausdierks.com;

Find A Grave, www.findagrave.com;

Fitzner, Rudolf, *Deutsches Kolonial-Handbuch* (Berlin: H. Pätel, 1901)

Gall, Sandy, *The Bushmen of Southern Africa* (London: Random House, 1910);

Genealogical Society of South Africa, www.eggsa.org;

German Colonial Uniforms, 'Aircraft in the German Colonies', http://s400910952.websitehome.co.uk/germancolonialuniforms/hist%20 0aircraft.htm;

Gewald, Jan-Bart, *Herero Heroes: A Socio-Political History of the Herero of Namibia 1890-1923* (Oxford: James Currey 1999);

Johannesburg Heritage, *Alfred August Hoheisen (1878-1965) early Johannesburg builder*, by Mike Bosazza, http://joburgheritage.co.za;

Kaasbøll, Jens, *Genealogy Luderitz, Namibia 1909-1919*, http://heim.ifi.uio.no/~jensj/Slekt/Luderitz/index.html;

Levinson, Olga, *Diamonds in the Desert: the story of August Stauch and his times* (Cape Town: Tafelberg, 1983);

Mahnecke, J.O.E.O., 'Aircraft operations in the German Colonies, 1911-1916; The *Fliegertruppe* of the Imperial German Army', *Military History Journal*, South African Military History Society, Vol. 12, No. 2, 2001;

Marais, Chris and Du Toit, Julienne, *Namibia Space* (Cape Town: Struik, 2006);

Moser, Jana, *Untersuchungen zur Kartographiegeschichte von Namibia: Die Entwicklung des Karten- und Vermessungswesens von den Anfängen bis zur Unabhängigkeit 1990* (Doctoral dissertation, Dresden: University of Dresden, 1990);

Oosthuizen, G.J.J., 'The military role of the Rehoboth Basters during the South African invasion of German South-West Africa, 1914-1915', *Scientia Militaria*, Vol. 28, No. 1, 1998.

Prothero, G.W. (ed), *Treatment of Natives in the German Colonies* (London: H.M. Stationery Office, 1920);

Southern Africa Association for the Advancement of Science, *S2A3 Biographical Database of Southern African Science*, www.s2a3.org.za;

Spieker, Johannes, *Mein Tagebuch: Erfahrungen eines deutschen Missionars in Deutsch–Südwestafrika 1905-1907* (Berlin, Germany: Simon-Verl. für Bibliothekswissen, 2013);

Steenken, Helmuth, *Kult Sammlung Stammeskunst*, www.kult-sammlung-stammeskunst.de;

Tonchi, Victor and others, *Historical Dictionary of Namibia* (Lanham, MD: Scarecrow Press, 2012);

Unknown, *Koloniales Hand- und Adreßbuch 1926-1927* (Berlin: Verlag Kolonialkriegerdank E.V., 1926);

Wikipedia, The Free Encyclopedia, www.wikipedia.org;

Index